The *Children's* *Baking* Book

LONDON, NEW YORK, MUNICH,
MELBOURNE, AND DELHI

Project Editor Heather Scott
Senior Designer Lisa Sodeau
Editor Julia March
Home Economist Denise Smart
Managing Editor Catherine Saunders
Art Director Lisa Lanzarini
Publishing Manager Simon Beecroft
Category Publisher Alex Allan
Production Controller Nick Seston
Senior Production Editor Clare McLean
US Editor Margaret Parrish

First published in the United States in 2009 by
DK Publishing
375 Hudson Street, New York, New York 10014

09 10 11 12 13 10 9 8 7 6 5 4 3 2 1
CD305—12/09

A catalog record for this book is available from the Library of Congress.
ISBN: 978-0-7566-5788-8

Reproduced in the UK by MDP
Printed and bound in China by Toppan

Acknowledgments

The publisher would like to thank the following young
chefs for their help in making this book so much fun:
Shannon Vass and Sophia O'Donohue. Thanks also to
photography assistant Ria Osborne.

Discover more at
www.dk.com

Recipes & Styling by Denise Smart
Photography by Howard Shooter

Contents

page 54

★ *Introduction* 6-7

page 44

page 76

page 96

page 112

page 116

page 94

Introduction

It is so satisfying to eat food you have cooked yourself, and baking is one of the most enjoyable methods of cooking. Baking uses lots of great techniques and delicious ingredients and, best of all, it fills your kitchen with the most wonderful smells!

Safe baking

Baking is lots of fun, but with heat and sharp objects around you must always take care to be safe and sensible.

- Use oven mitts when handling hot pans, baking sheets, or dishes.
- Don't put hot pans or trays directly onto the work surface—use a heat-proof trivet, mat, rack, or board.
- When you are stirring food on the stove, grip the handle firmly to steady the pan.
- When cooking on a burner, turn the pan handles to the side (away from the heat and the front) so that you are less likely to knock them over.
- Be extra careful on any step where you see the warning triangle symbol.

Getting started

1. Read the recipe through before you begin.
2. Wash your hands, tie your hair back (if necessary), and put on an apron.
3. Gather all the ingredients and equipment you need.
4. Start baking!

How to use the spreads

There's a lot of information packed onto each page, so here's how to get the best out of the recipes. You'll find simple instructions, tips, delicious variations, and mouthwatering recipes.

The lists of tools and ingredients tell you everything you will need.

The introduction tells you a bit about the recipe.

This tells you the level of difficulty and the color indicates which section of the book the recipe is in.

Check here for the quantity the recipe makes or how many it serves and how long it will take.

The chef's tip will give you some useful cooking advice.

Step-by-step pictures and text will guide you through the recipes.

Many of the recipes can be adapted to make different flavors.

After safety, cleanliness is the most important thing to be aware of in the kitchen. Here are a few simple hygiene rules for you to follow:

- Always wash your hands before you start baking, and after handling raw meat.
- Wash all fruits and vegetables.
- Use separate cutting boards for meat and vegetables.
- Keep your cooking area clean and have a cloth handy to wipe up any spills.
- Store cooked and raw food separately.
- Always check the use-by date on all ingredients. Do not use them if the date has passed.
- Keep meat in the refrigerator until you need it and always make sure to cook it thoroughly.

Cookies and Baked Goods

In this section there are lots of delicious recipes for individual baked treats. Cookies and baked goods are very easy to make, and, because they often don't take long to bake, they are perfect for a quick baking session.

Mixing

Mixing means putting ingredients together. You can do this by hand, or with a spoon, whisk, electric mixer, or food processor.

Top Tip

When you are cutting out shapes for cookies, cut out as many as you can and then gather up the scraps and roll them out again. Repeat until you have used up all the dough and none is wasted.

Rolling and cutting out

When rolling out dough with a rolling pin, make sure the work surface and the rolling pin are sprinkled with flour to prevent the dough from sticking. When cutting out shapes, gently wiggle the pastry or cookie cutter from side to side—you will find it lifts out easily.

Top Tip

Always use unsalted butter unless the recipe tells you otherwise. Salted butter burns more easily and is less healthy.

Measuring

Measuring out ingredients is important. The ingredients in these recipes have been carefully calculated so that the finished baked goods turn out just right. The amounts needed are given in Imperial and metric measurements. Always stick to one version.

Storage

If you have any leftovers or want to save your creations for later, put them in a sealed, airtight container to keep them fresh.

Toffee Squares

These toffee squares are yummy! For extra stickiness, the squares are topped with a caramel toffee sauce. You can buy this in a jar, but it's more fun to make your own.

Flour

Eggs

Palette knife

Tools

- 11" x 7" (28 cm x 18 cm) pan
- Parchment paper
- Small saucepan
- Large mixing bowl
- Electric mixer or whisk
- Metal spoon
- Oven mitts
- Cooling rack
- Cutting board
- Sharp knife
- Palette knife

Saucepan

Ingredients

- 1 cup (150 g) pitted soft dates (roughly chopped)
- 4 fl oz (125 ml) cold water
- 1 tsp baking soda
- 5 oz (150 g) butter (softened)
- 1 cup (150 g) dark brown sugar
- 2 medium eggs (beaten)
- 1 tsp vanilla extract
- 1½ cups (175 g) self-rising flour

Toffee topping
- 6 tbsp caramel toffee sauce (Dulce de Leche)

Sugar

Dates

Chef's Tip

These squares taste delicious served warm with ice cream drizzled with caramel sauce.

1 Preheat the oven to 350°F (180°C). Lightly grease an 11" x 7" (28 cm x 18 cm) pan and line the bottom with parchment paper to prevent the cake from sticking.

2 Place the dates in a pan and add the water. Bring to a boil, then remove from the heat and add the baking soda—the mixture will fizz! Leave to one side to cool slightly.

3 Place the butter and sugar in a large mixing bowl. Using an electric mixer or whisk, beat them together until they are light and fluffy. Beat in the eggs and vanilla extract.

4 Using a metal spoon, fold in the flour, then the date mixture. Pour the mixture into the pan. Place the pan in the center of the oven and bake for 25–30 minutes, or until risen.

5 Allow the cake to cool in the pan for 10 minutes, then transfer it to a cooling rack. When cold, cut it into 24 squares, then spread your caramel sauce over the top with a palette knife.

Chef's Tip

To make your own caramel sauce, bring 3 oz (75 g) butter, ¾ cup (150 g) light brown sugar, and ½ cup (150 ml) table cream to a boil and cook for 3 minutes, until thickened. Allow to cool.

Chocolate and Cranberry Cookies

The perfect combination of tart cranberries and sweet white chocolate makes these cookies melt in your mouth!

Makes

15

Prep

10 mins

Cooking

15 mins

Chef's Tip

Eat these yummy cookies while they are still warm—since the chocolate will be gooey. Delicious!

Tools

- Two baking sheets
- Parchment paper
- Large mixing bowl
- Electric mixer or whisk
- Dessert spoon
- Oven mitts
- Cooling rack
- Spatula

Electric mixer

Sugar

Butter

Large mixing bowl

Ingredients

- 4 oz (125 g) butter (softened)
- 2/3 cup (125 g) light brown sugar
- 1 medium egg (beaten)
- 1 tbsp milk
- 1¼ cups (150 g) all-purpose flour
- ½ tsp baking powder
- 2 oz (50g) white chocolate (finely grated)
- 2/3 cup (100 g) white chocolate chips
- 2 oz (50 g) dried cranberries

Flour

Dried cranberries

Milk

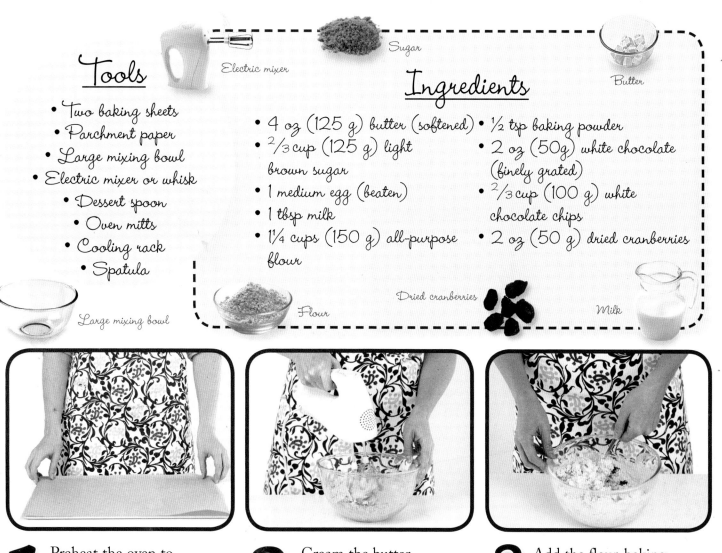

1 Preheat the oven to 375°F (180°C). Line two baking sheets with parchment paper to prevent the cookies from sticking while they are baking.

2 Cream the butter and sugar together in a large bowl until pale. (You can use a whisk or electric mixer.) Then beat in the egg and milk.

3 Add the flour, baking powder, grated chocolate, white chocolate chips, and cranberries to the mixture. Using a large spoon, stir until they are thoroughly mixed together.

4 Place spoonfuls of the cookie mixture onto the prepared baking sheets. Leave space in between, so the cookies do not touch as they cook.

5 Bake for 12–15 minutes, until lightly golden and slightly soft to the touch. Allow to cool on the baking sheet for 5 minutes, then transfer to a cooling rack to cool completely.

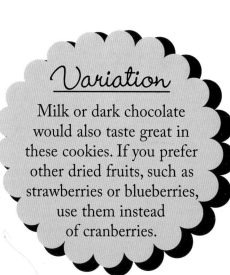

Variation

Milk or dark chocolate would also taste great in these cookies. If you prefer other dried fruits, such as strawberries or blueberries, use them instead of cranberries.

Medium

Makes 20

Prep 40 mins

Cooking 25 mins

Cheesy Shortbread

These light and buttery cheese treats make a perfect afternoon snack. Or serve them at a party and watch them disappear!

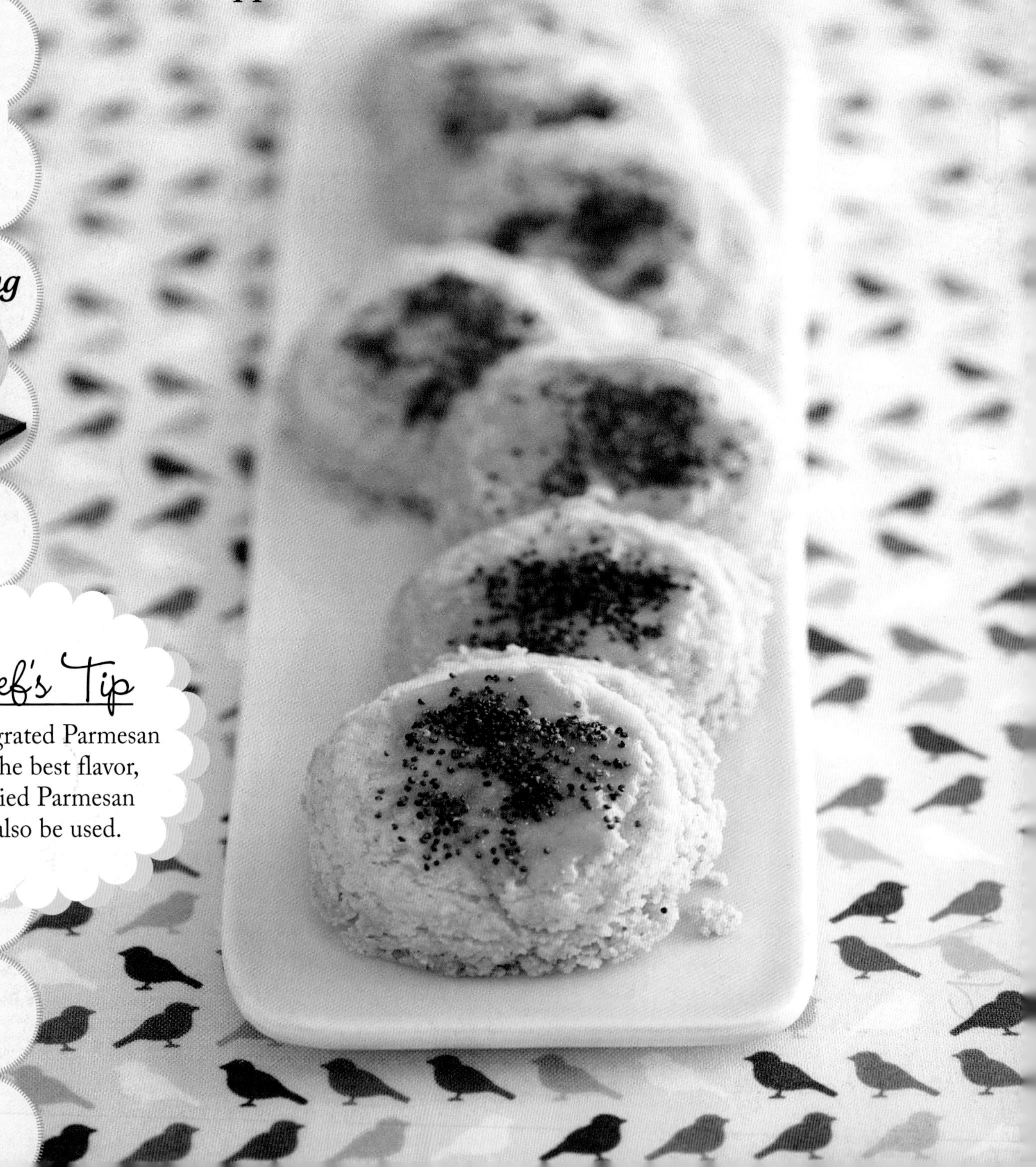

Chef's Tip

Freshly grated Parmesan gives the best flavor, but dried Parmesan can also be used.

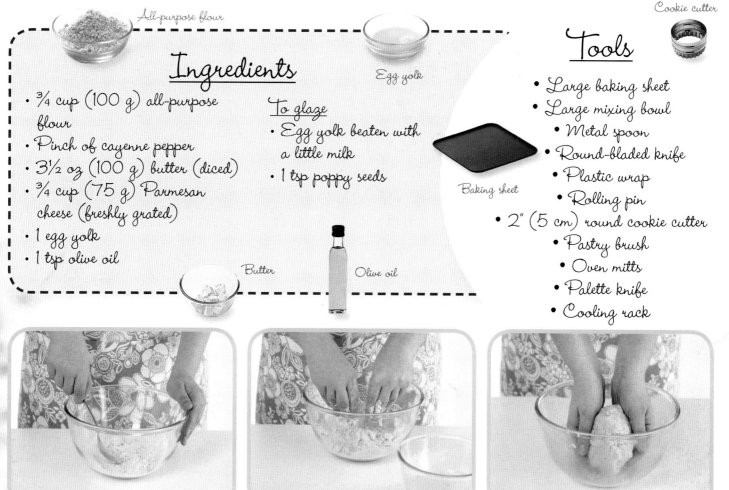

Ingredients

- ¾ cup (100 g) all-purpose flour
- Pinch of cayenne pepper
- 3½ oz (100 g) butter (diced)
- ¾ cup (75 g) Parmesan cheese (freshly grated)
- 1 egg yolk
- 1 tsp olive oil

All-purpose flour

Egg yolk

To glaze
- Egg yolk beaten with a little milk
- 1 tsp poppy seeds

Butter

Olive oil

Baking sheet

Cookie cutter

Tools

- Large baking sheet
- Large mixing bowl
- Metal spoon
- Round-bladed knife
- Plastic wrap
- Rolling pin
- 2" (5 cm) round cookie cutter
- Pastry brush
- Oven mitts
- Palette knife
- Cooling rack

1 Lightly grease a large baking sheet with butter. Preheat the oven to 325°F (170°C). Place the flour and cayenne pepper in a large mixing bowl and mix together with a metal spoon.

2 Add the butter to the flour mixture. Rub it in using your fingertips until the mixture resembles breadcrumbs. Then stir in the Parmesan cheese with a metal spoon.

3 Add the egg yolk and olive oil and stir the mixture together with a round-bladed knife. Using your hands, form the mixture into a ball of dough. Wrap it in plastic wrap and chill for 30 minutes.

4 Using a floured rolling pin, roll out the chilled dough on a lightly floured surface to ½" (5 mm) thick. Using a 2" (5 cm) round cookie cutter, cut out 16 circles. Put them on the baking sheet.

5 Brush the tops of the circles with the egg yolk glaze and then sprinkle them with the poppy seeds. Bake them on the top shelf for 20–25 minutes, or until golden.

6 Leave the shortbread to cool on the baking sheet for a few minutes. Then, using a palette knife, transfer them to a cooling rack to cool completely.

No-bake Chocolate Squares

These crunchy, chocolatey fruit-and-nut squares couldn't be easier to make— they don't even need to be baked!

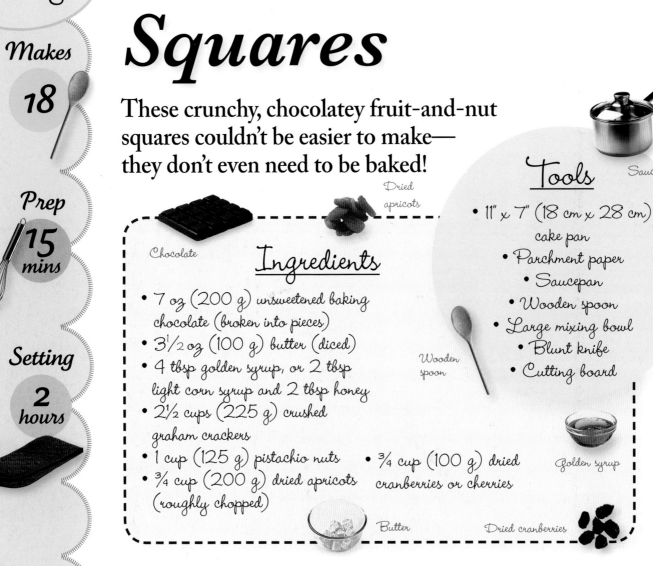

Chocolate

Dried apricots

Ingredients

- 7 oz (200 g) unsweetened baking chocolate (broken into pieces)
- 3½ oz (100 g) butter (diced)
- 4 tbsp golden syrup, or 2 tbsp light corn syrup and 2 tbsp honey
- 2½ cups (225 g) crushed graham crackers
- 1 cup (125 g) pistachio nuts
- ¾ cup (200 g) dried apricots (roughly chopped)
- ¾ cup (100 g) dried cranberries or cherries

Wooden spoon

Butter

Dried cranberries

Tools

Saucepan

- 11" x 7" (18 cm x 28 cm) cake pan
- Parchment paper
- Saucepan
- Wooden spoon
- Large mixing bowl
- Blunt knife
- Cutting board

Golden syrup

Chef's Tip

For a citrus twist, add the grated zest of an orange to the chocolate, butter, and golden syrup mixture.

1 Line an 11" x 7" (18 cm x 28 cm) pan with parchment paper. Place the chocolate, butter, and golden syrup in a saucepan over a low heat. Stir until melted and smooth.

2 Place all the remaining ingredients in a large mixing bowl and mix well. Pour over the chocolate mixture and stir until all the ingredients are evenly coated.

3 Pour the mixture into the prepared pan and spread it evenly with the back of a spoon. Chill for at least 2 hours or until firm to the touch.

4 Run a blunt knife around the edge of the pan. Carefully turn out onto a cutting board and remove the parchment paper. Cut into squares and serve.

Variation
You can replace the dried cranberries or cherries with the same quantity of currants, raisins, candied cherries, or prunes.

Rocky Road Cookies

Makes 14

Prep 10 mins

Cooking 11 mins

These gorgeous cookies are topped with chunky chocolate and melted marshmallows. The chunky and smooth textures are a perfect combination—yum!

Palette knife

Tools

- Two baking sheets
- Parchment paper
- Large mixing bowl
- Electric mixer or whisk
- Metal spoon
- Dessert spoon
- Oven mitts
- Palette knife
- Cooling rack

Chocolate

Brown sugar

Large mixing bowl

Ingredients

- 4 oz (125 g) butter (softened)
- ¾ cup (125 g) soft brown sugar
- 1 medium egg (beaten)
- 2 oz (50 g) milk chocolate (chopped)
- 1 cup (125 g) all-purpose flour
- 1 tbsp cocoa powder
- ½ tsp baking powder
- 2 oz (50 g) white chocolate (chopped)
- ½ cup (25 g) mini marshmallows

Egg

Flour

1 Preheat the oven to 375°F (180°C). Line two baking sheets with parchment paper. Use an electric mixer or whisk to cream the butter and sugar together in a mixing bowl.

2 Beat in the egg and milk. Then stir in the flour, cocoa powder, baking powder, and half the chunks of milk and white chocolate using a metal spoon.

3 Place spoonfuls of the mixture onto the prepared baking sheets, spacing them well apart. Flatten slightly and bake for 5 minutes, until the edges are starting to get firm.

4 Remove the cookies from the oven. Immediately sprinkle them with the marshmallows and remaining chocolate chunks, pressing them down into the cookies.

5 Return the cookies to the oven for a further 5–6 minutes or until slightly soft to the touch. Allow them to cool for 5 minutes, then transfer them to a cooling rack.

Variation

Experiment with different flavored chocolate chunks. Or try heart-shaped marshmallows for a Valentine's Day treat!

Raisin Cookies

These simply scrumptious cookies are sure to become a favorite. They are perfect for an afternoon snack or a light dessert.

Makes

20

Prep

20 mins

Cooking

14 mins

Variation

Replace the raisins with dried cranberries, if you prefer, or spice things up by adding a little cinnamon, nutmeg, or allspice.

Ingredients

- 4 oz (125 g) butter (softened)
- ⅓ cup (75 g) sugar
- Finely grated zest of 1 lemon
- 1 egg (separated)
- 1⅔ cups (200 g) all-purpose flour (sifted)
- ½ cup (75 g) raisins
- 2 tbsp milk
- 1–2 tbsp sugar (for sprinkling)

Butter

Egg

Lemon

Raisins

Electric mixer

Pastry brush

Tools

- Two large baking sheets
- Large mixing bowl
- Electric mixer or whisk
- Round-bladed knife
- Rolling pin
- 2½" (6 cm) round fluted cookie cutter
- Oven mitts
- Fork
- Pastry brush
- Palette knife
- Cooling rack

1 Preheat the oven to 350°F (180°C). Grease two baking sheets. In a bowl, beat the butter, sugar, and lemon zest together using an electric mixer or whisk, until they are pale and fluffy.

2 Beat in the egg yolk but keep the egg white to one side. Using a round-bladed knife, gently stir in the sifted flour and raisins. Gradually stir in the milk until the dough comes together.

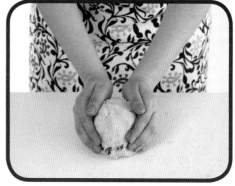

3 Place the dough on a lightly floured surface and knead it gently until it is smooth and supple. Shape the dough into a ball with your hands.

4 Roll the dough out to about ¼" (5 mm) thick then cut out the cookies using a 2½" (6 cm) round fluted cookie cutter. Place the cookies on the baking sheets and bake for 8–10 minutes.

5 Using oven mitts, remove the baking sheets from the oven. Lightly whisk the egg white with a fork, then brush it over the cookies with a pastry brush and sprinkle them with sugar.

6 Wearing the oven mitts, return the cookies to the oven for 3–4 minutes, or until they turn golden. Once cooked, remove the cookies from the oven and transfer them to a cooling rack.

Melting Moments

These melt-in-your-mouth cookies are a chocolate-lover's dream! The creamy filling and crunchy cookie make a tasty combination.

Makes 15

Prep 20 mins

Cooking 15 mins

Tools

- Two large baking sheets
- Parchment paper
- Large mixing bowl
- Electric mixer or wooden spoon
- Sifter
- Metal spoon
- Teaspoon
- Oven mitts
- Cooling rack
- Palette knife
- Heat-proof bowl
- Small saucepan
- Wooden spoon

Heat-proof bowl

Butter

Ingredients

- 6 oz (175 g) butter (softened)
- ¼ cup (50 g) sugar
- 1 tsp vanilla extract
- 1 cup (125 g) all-purpose flour
- 3 tbsp (25 g) cornstarch
- ¼ cup (25 g) cocoa powder (sifted)

For the filling
- 4 oz (100 g) good quality chocolate (broken into pieces)
- 2 tbsp heavy cream

Baking sheet

Chocolate

Sugar

All-purpose flour

1 Preheat the oven to 350°F (180°C). Line two baking sheets with parchment paper. Place the butter, sugar, and vanilla extract in a bowl; beat with an electric mixer, whisk, or wooden spoon.

2 Sift the flour, cornstarch, and cocoa powder into the mixing bowl. Using a metal spoon, fold them into the mixture until the ingredients are well combined.

3 Using a teaspoon, spoon 15 dollops, each about 1" (2.5 cm) round, onto the baking sheets, so you have 30 in total. Allow room between the cookies, since they will spread while cooking.

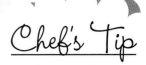

Chef's Tip

For a perfect, professional finish, use a piping bag with a star-shaped nozzle in Step 3. See page 123 for tips on how to make your own piping bag.

4 Bake for 12–15 minutes, or until the cookies are just starting to become dark around the edges. Remove them from the oven and leave to cool slightly before moving to a cooling rack.

5 Place the chocolate and cream in a heat-proof bowl over a saucepan of simmering water. Stir them until they have melted. Remove from the heat and leave to cool completely.

6 Using a palette knife, spread the filling on the flat side of half of the cooled cookies and sandwich each one with one of the remaining cookies.

Jam Shapes

These pretty jam-filled cookies take time to make, but they are definitely worth the effort! The combination of gooey jam and crunchy cookie is heavenly.

1 Preheat the oven to 325°F (170°C). Line two baking sheets with parchment paper. Process the butter, sugar, vanilla extract, and lemon zest in a food processor until smooth.

2 Add the egg, egg yolk, and flour to the food processor and process again until the mixture resembles breadcrumbs and is starting to come together in a dough.

3 Transfer the dough to a lightly floured surface and lightly knead until it is smooth. Flatten into a circle, wrap it in plastic wrap, and chill for 30 minutes.

Ingredients

- 6 oz (175 g) butter (softened)
- 7/8 cup (175 g) sugar
- 1 tsp vanilla extract
- 1 tsp finely grated lemon zest
- 1 medium egg (beaten)
- 1 egg yolk
- 2¼ cups (275 g) all-purpose flour, plus a little extra for rolling out
- 6 tbsp raspberry or strawberry jam
- 2 tbsp confectioners' sugar (for dusting)

Eggs

Sugar

Food processor

Lemon

Butter

Oven mitts

Tools

Rolling pin

- Two large baking sheets
- Parchment paper
- Food processor
- Plastic wrap
- Rolling pin
- 2½" (6 cm) cookie cutter
- 1–1½" (2–3 cm) cookie cutter
- Oven mitts
- Cooling rack
- Palette knife

Chef's Tip

Use different shaped cookie cutters for different shaped cookies. Make sure that any cookie cutter you use has a smaller version for the hole in the middle.

4 On a lightly floured surface, roll the dough out to ¼" (3 mm) thick. Using a 2½" (6 cm) cookie cutter, cut out as many cookies as you can. You should get about 36 in total.

5 Use a 1–1½" (2–3 cm) cookie cutter to cut out the middle from 18 of the cookies (you can bake these too if you like). Arrange on the baking sheets and chill for 15 minutes.

6 Bake on the middle shelf of the oven (in batches, if necessary) for about 10–12 minutes, or until golden. Cool on the baking sheets for 1 minute, then transfer the cookies to a cooling rack.

7 When fully cool, spread the whole cookies with jam. Then dust confectioners' sugar on the cookies with holes. Press one sugar-dusted cookie onto each jam-covered one and serve.

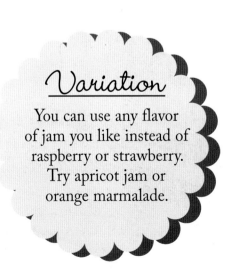

Variation

You can use any flavor of jam you like instead of raspberry or strawberry. Try apricot jam or orange marmalade.

Easy

Makes
20

Prep
10
mins

Cooking
15
mins

Cheesy Oatcakes

These crunchy, savory cookies are delicious served warm or cold. They are perfect for a snack or a light lunch. Serve them with your favorite cheese and some salad.

Variation

If you don't like rosemary just leave it out. Alternatively, you could add 1 tsp dried mixed herbs.

Ingredients

- 1½ cups (225 g) oatmeal
- ½ cup (50 g) Cheddar cheese (finely grated)
- ½ tsp salt
- ½ tsp baking soda
- 1 tsp paprika (optional)
- 2 tsp freshly chopped rosemary (optional)
- 1 oz (25 g) butter (melted)
- 1 egg yolk
- 4 tbsp warm water

Egg yolk

Cheese

Salt

Butter

Tools

- Large baking sheet
- Large mixing bowl
- Wooden spoon
- Rolling pin
- 2½" (6 cm) cookie cutter
- Oven mitts

Oven mitts

Rolling pin

Baking sheet

1 Preheat the oven to 400°F (200°C). Lightly grease a large baking sheet with some butter and cover it with a piece of parchment paper to prevent the oatcakes from sticking.

2 Place the oatmeal, cheese, salt, baking soda, paprika, and rosemary in a large mixing bowl. Stir the ingredients together with a wooden spoon until they are mixed.

3 Stir in the butter, egg yolk, and water to make a sticky dough. Place the dough on a lightly floured surface and use your hands to press the mixture together.

4 Roll out the dough to about ⅛" (2 mm) thick on a lightly floured surface. Using a 2½" (6 cm) cookie cutter, cut out the cookies. Gather up the trimmings and reroll and cut out.

5 Place the cookies on the baking sheet. Place the sheet in the top of the oven and bake for 15 minutes. Remove the baking sheet from the oven and let the oatcakes cool completely.

Chef's Tip
You can store the oatcakes in an airtight container for up to a week. Don't keep them any longer or they will start to get soft.

Orange Sunflower Cookies

These oaty cookies are flavored with tangy orange. The sunflower seeds are a great source of vitamins and minerals, as well as adding an extra crunch!

Makes

14

Prep

15 mins

Cooking

10 mins

Chef's Tip

To make smaller cookies, place heaping teaspoonfuls instead of dessert spoonfuls of the mixture on the baking sheets and bake for 7–9 minutes.

Sunflower seeds

Orange

Rolled oats

Bowl

Ingredients

- 1 cup (125 g) rolled oats
- ½ cup (75 g) sunflower seeds
- 1¼ cups (150 g) self-rising flour
- 5 oz (150 g) butter (diced)
- Grated zest of 1 orange
- 2 tbsp orange juice
- 1 cup (150 g) light brown sugar
- 2 tbsp golden syrup, or 1 tbsp corn syrup and 1 tbsp honey

Tools

- Three large baking sheets
- Parchment paper
- Large mixing bowl
- Wooden spoon
- Medium saucepan
- Dessert spoon
- Oven mitts
- Cooling rack
- Palette knife

Wooden spoon

Butter

Golden syrup

Baking sheet

1 Preheat the oven to 350°F (180°C). Line three large baking sheets with parchment paper to prevent the cookies from sticking to them.

2 Place the oats, sunflower seeds, and flour in a large mixing bowl. Stir the mixture with a wooden spoon until completely mixed together. Put the bowl to one side.

3 Place the butter, orange zest, juice, sugar, and golden syrup in a medium saucepan. Heat the mixture over a low heat while stirring, until the butter and sugar have melted.

4 Carefully pour the butter mixture over the ingredients in the large mixing bowl and mix them together with the wooden spoon until thoroughly combined.

5 Place heaping dessert spoonfuls of the mixture onto each sheet. Leave a generous space between the cookies, since they will spread. Bake for 8–10 minutes, until golden.

6 Leave the cookies to cool on the sheet for a few minutes, then transfer them to a cooling rack with a palette knife, to become crisp. They will keep in an airtight container for 2–3 days.

Star Cookies

These cookies make great gifts for your friends and family. You can use different shaped cookie cutters for different themes, such as Christmas, Halloween, or Valentine's Day.

Makes
15

Prep
25 mins

Cooking
12 mins

Chef's Tip
You can hang these cookies as pretty decorations. Use a skewer to make holes and thread them with ribbons.

Ingredients

Butter

Beaten egg

- 1²/₃ cups (200 g) all-purpose flour
- 4 oz (125 g) butter (diced)
- ½ cup (100 g) sugar
- 1 tsp ground cinnamon
- Finely grated zest of 1 orange

- 1 medium egg, lightly beaten
- 2 tbsp golden syrup, or 1 tbsp corn syrup and 1 tbsp honey

To decorate: ribbon, writing icing, edible silver balls, or sprinkles

Flour

Orange

Golden syrup

Tools

- Two large baking sheets
- Parchment paper
- Food processor
- Small bowl
- Fork   Skewers
- Rolling pin
- Star-shaped cookie cutter
- Skewer
- Oven mitts
- Cooling rack

Food processor

1 Preheat the oven to 350°F (180°C). Line two large baking sheets with parchment paper. Mix the flour and butter in a food processor, until the mixture resembles fine breadcrumbs.

2 Add the sugar, cinnamon, and orange zest and mix again. In a small bowl, beat together the egg and golden syrup with a fork, then add this to the breadcrumb mixture.

3 Process the mixture in the food processor until it comes together in a ball. Lift the ball of dough out, wrap it in plastic wrap, and chill for 10 minutes in the refrigerator.

4 Roll out the chilled dough on a lightly floured surface, to ¼" (4–5mm) thickness. Cut into stars using a star-shaped cookie cutter. Reroll; cut out more stars until you use up all the dough.

5 Place the stars slightly apart on the baking sheets and cook for 10–12 minutes. Allow to cool for 2 minutes and, if they are decorations, poke a hole in the top of each using the skewer.

6 Place the stars on a cooling rack. When they are cool, decorate them as desired. Thread the holes with ribbon and tie the ends together if you will be using the stars as decorations.

Granola Bars

Tasty crumbly oats mixed with sticky, sweet syrup and crunchy corn flakes make these granola bars completely irresistible. Oats release energy slowly, so after eating one of these bars you won't feel hungry for a while.

Makes

16

Prep

10
mins

Cooking

25
mins

Chef's Tip

Don't be tempted to take the granola bars out of the pan until they are completely cooled or they will break apart.

Ingredients

- 6 oz (175 g) butter (diced)
- 1¼ cups (175 g) light brown sugar
- 4 tbsp golden syrup, or 2 tbsp light corn syrup and 2 tbsp honey
- 2¼ cups (350 g) whole rolled oats
- 2 cups (50 g) corn flakes

Sugar

Rolled oats

Butter

Golden syrup

Tools

- Large saucepan
- Wooden spoon
- 11" x 7" (28 cm x 18 cm) pan
- Oven mitts
- Sharp knife

Knife

Oven mitts

Saucepan

Chef's Tip

Cut the granola bars into squares while they are still slightly warm, otherwise they will be too hard to cut.

1 Preheat the oven to 350°F (180°C). In a saucepan, gently melt the butter, sugar, and golden syrup over a low heat, stirring with a wooden spoon until the sugar has dissolved.

2 Remove the saucepan from the heat and gently stir in the rolled oats and the corn flakes with the wooden spoon, until the mixture is thoroughly combined and sticky.

3 Pour the mixture into an 11" x 7" (28 cm x 18 cm) pan and spread it into the corners. Gently press down with the back of the wooden spoon to make the top flat and even.

4 Bake the mixture for 25 minutes, or until golden and firm. Allow to cool for 10 minutes, then cut it into bars. Leave to cool completely before lifting the bars out of the pan.

Variation

You can add ⅓ cup (50 g) dried fruit, such as chopped apricots, dried cranberries, blueberries, or raisins for fruity granola bars.

Ginger and Pumpkin Slices

This sticky pumpkin and ginger cake is wonderfully dark and moist. It tastes even better the day after baking—if you can resist eating it for that long!

Makes

18

Prep

15
mins

Cooking

40
mins

Golden syrup

Ingredients

Butter

- 4 oz (125 g) butter
- ½ cup (75 g) dark brown sugar
- ½ cup (150 g) golden syrup, or ¼ cup corn syrup and ¼ cup honey
- ½ cup (150 g) dark molasses
- 2 cups (250 g) grated pumpkin
- 2½ cups (300 g) all-purpose flour
- 1 tsp baking soda
- 2 tsp ground ginger
- Two medium eggs (beaten)

Flour

Sugar

Square cake pan

Tools

- 9" (23 cm) square cake pan
- Parchment paper
- Medium saucepan
- Wooden spoon
- Large mixing bowl
- Oven mitts
- Cutting board
- Sharp knife

Oven mitts

Variation

If pumpkins are not in season, use grated butternut squash instead. The two have a similar flavor, since they are both part of the squash family of vegetables.

1 Grease the bottom of a 9" (23 cm) square cake pan with a pat of butter on some parchment paper and line the pan with parchment paper. Preheat the oven to 350°F (180°C).

2 Place the butter, sugar, golden syrup, and molasses in a medium pan and heat gently until the sugar has dissolved and the butter has melted. Remove from the heat and allow to cool.

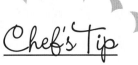

Chef's Tip
This cake tastes even
better after a few days.
Wrap it in wax paper and
keep it in an airtight
container for up to
a week.

3 In a large mixing bowl, add the grated pumpkin or butternut squash, flour, baking soda, and ginger. Mix thoroughly with a wooden spoon.

4 Stir in the molasses mixture and beaten eggs until combined, then pour into the greased and lined pan. Bake in the middle of the oven for 35–40 minutes, or until firm.

5 Allow the cake to cool in the pan. Once cool, carefully transfer it onto a cutting board. Peel the paper off the back and, using a sharp knife, cut the cake into rectangles.

Coconut Cookies

Give oat cookies a tasty tropical twist with creamy coconut. The baking soda gives the cookies a great crunchy texture.

Makes

20

Prep

10 mins

Cooking

10 mins

Ingredients

Flour

- 1 cup (75 g) dried coconut
- ¾ cup (100 g) all-purpose flour
- ½ cup (100 g) sugar
- ¾ cup (100 g) rolled oats
- 3½ oz (100 g) butter (diced)
- 1 tbsp golden syrup, or ½ tbsp light corn syrup and ½ tbsp honey
- 1 tsp baking soda
- 2 tbsp hot water

Large mixing bowl

Rolled oats

Butter

Tools

Wooden spoon

- Two baking sheets
- Parchment paper
- Large mixing bowl
- Wooden spoon
- Medium saucepan
- Dessert spoon
- Oven mitts
- Palette knife
- Cooling rack

Saucepan

Chef's Tip

These cookies will store for up to a week in an airtight container.

1 Preheat the oven to 350°F (180°C). Line two baking sheets with parchment paper. Place the coconut, flour, sugar, and oats in a mixing bowl and mix together with a wooden spoon.

2 Place the butter and golden syrup in a medium saucepan and heat over a low heat until melted. Stir the mixture with a wooden spoon to mix thoroughly.

3 Mix the baking soda with the hot water. Add it to the butter mixture in the saucepan. The baking soda will make the butter and golden syrup mixture fizz. Stir well.

4 Pour the butter mixture into the large mixing bowl and mix well. Spoon the mixture onto the baking sheets, leaving room between each one for the cookies to spread.

5 Bake the cookies for 8–10 minutes on the top shelf of the oven until golden. Allow the cookies to cool on the sheet for 5 minutes, then transfer to a cooling rack to cool completely.

Medium

Makes 36

Prep 20 mins

Cooking 25 mins

Chocolate Fudge Brownies

These delicious brownies are perfect—crisp on the outside and fudgy on the inside. Be careful not to overcook them—they should be gooey in the middle.

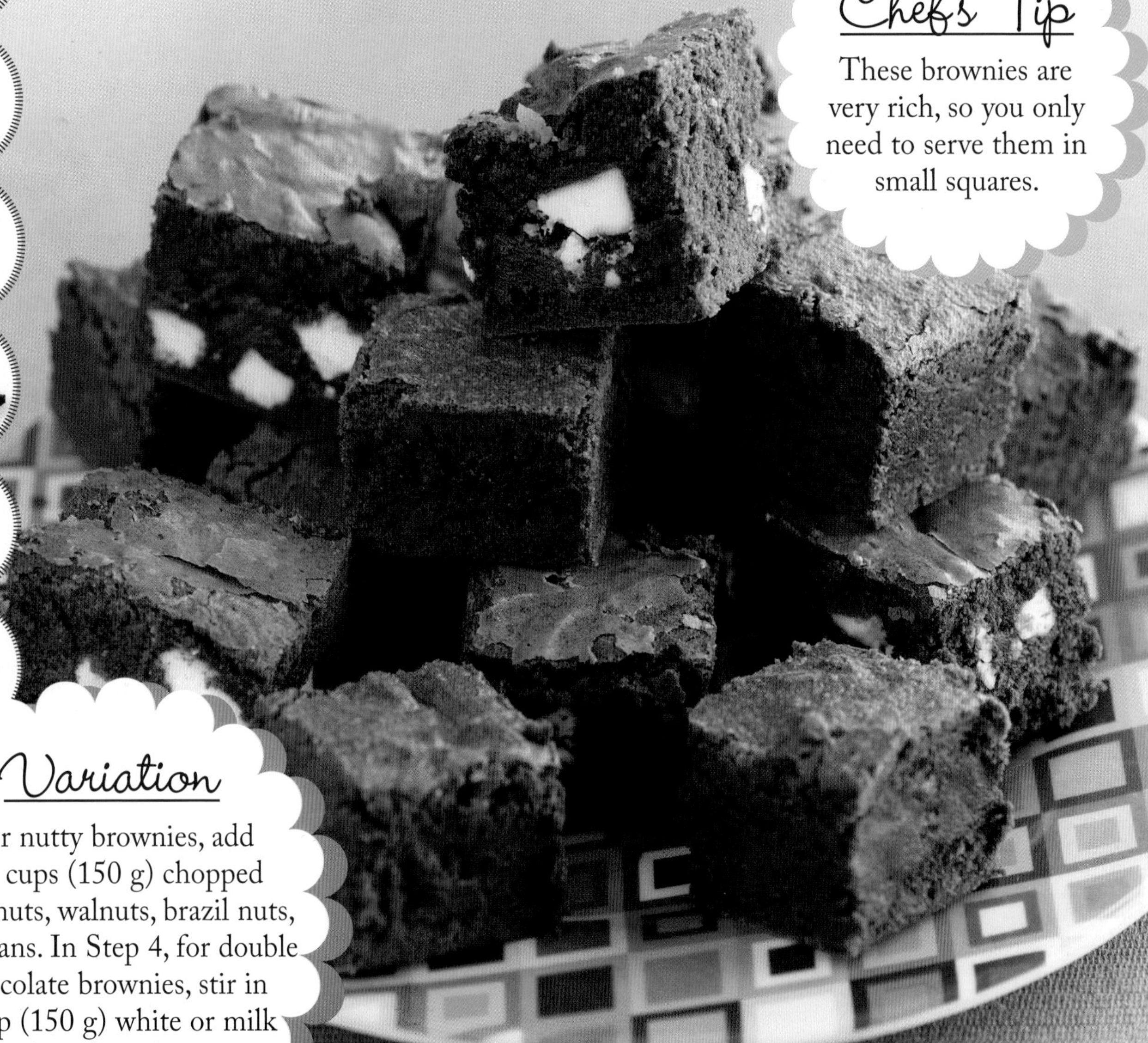

Chef's Tip

These brownies are very rich, so you only need to serve them in small squares.

Variation

For nutty brownies, add 1⅓ cups (150 g) chopped hazelnuts, walnuts, brazil nuts, or pecans. In Step 4, for double chocolate brownies, stir in 1 cup (150 g) white or milk chocolate chips.

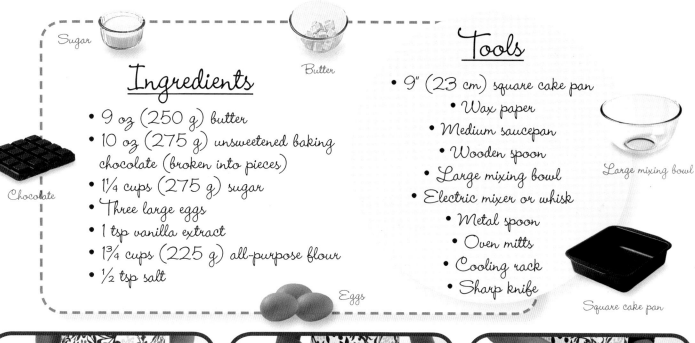

Ingredients

Sugar

Butter

- 9 oz (250 g) butter
- 10 oz (275 g) unsweetened baking chocolate (broken into pieces)
- 1¼ cups (275 g) sugar
- Three large eggs
- 1 tsp vanilla extract
- 1¾ cups (225 g) all-purpose flour
- ½ tsp salt

Chocolate

Eggs

Tools

- 9" (23 cm) square cake pan
- Wax paper
- Medium saucepan
- Wooden spoon
- Large mixing bowl
- Electric mixer or whisk
- Metal spoon
- Oven mitts
- Cooling rack
- Sharp knife

Large mixing bowl

Square cake pan

1 Preheat the oven to 350°F (180°C). Grease and line the bottom of a 9" (23 cm) square cake pan with parchment paper to prevent the brownies from sticking.

2 Melt the butter and chocolate in a medium saucepan over a low heat, stirring occasionally with a wooden spoon. Remove the saucepan from the heat and allow to cool slightly.

3 In a large mixing bowl, beat together the sugar, eggs, and vanilla extract using an electric mixer or whisk. Keep mixing until the mixture is pale and fluffy.

4 Whisk the chocolate mixture into the egg mixture until thoroughly combined, using the electric mixer or whisk. Then stir in the flour and salt with a metal spoon.

5 Pour the mixture into the prepared pan and cook for 20–25 minutes in the middle of the oven, until the brownies are just set. The center should be slightly gooey.

6 Leave the cake to cool for 10 minutes in the pan. Place it on a cooling rack. When it is completely cold, remove the parchment paper and cut the brownies into squares.

Gingerbread

Gingerbread tastes great and smells wonderful as it bakes. This recipe can be used for regular-shaped cookies, pretty tree ornaments, or gingerbread people.

Makes
15

Prep
15 mins

Cooking
10 mins

Golden syrup

Large mixing bowl

Ingredients

- 3 cups (350 g) all-purpose flour
- 2 tsp ground ginger

- 1 tsp baking soda
- 4 oz (125 g) butter (diced)
- 1 cup (150 g) dark brown sugar
- 4 tbsp golden syrup, or 2 tbsp light corn syrup and 2 tbsp honey
- 1 medium egg (beaten)
- Candies, raisins, and icing for decoration

Tools

- Two large baking sheets
- Parchment paper
- Large mixing bowl
- Wooden spoon
- Rolling pin
- Cookie cutters
- Oven mitts

Wooden spoon

Butter

Sugar

Chef's Tip

These cookies can be stored in an airtight container for two days. To make them into decorations, use a skewer to punch a hole through the cookie once it's baked and thread a ribbon through the hole.

1 Preheat the oven to 350°F (180°C). Line two large baking sheets with parchment paper. If you only have one baking sheet, you will need to bake the cookies in two batches.

2 Place the flour, ginger, and baking soda in a large bowl. Stir the ingredients together with a wooden spoon until they are mixed thoroughly.

3 Rub the butter into the mixture using your fingertips. Continue rubbing in the butter until the mixture resembles fine breadcrumbs. Stir in the sugar.

4 Stir in the golden syrup and egg, until the mixture starts to come together into a dough. Place the dough mixture on a lightly floured surface and knead it until smooth.

5 Roll out the dough on a lightly floured surface to a thickness of ¼" (5 mm), then, using your cookie cutters, cut out the shapes. Reroll the leftover dough and cut out more cookies.

6 Place the cookies on the baking sheets and bake for 9–10 minutes, or until golden. Allow the cookies to cool on the sheets. Decorate with candies, raisins, and icing.

Doughs

Home-baked bread tastes fantastic and fills your kitchen with wonderful smells as it bakes! There are lots of special techniques you will need to know to bake your own bread. In this section you will learn all about the art and science of making dough.

Mixing

Dough is very sticky. Use a spoon or knife to mix it together at first, but then don't be afraid to roll up your sleeves and knead with your hands. It's lots of fun!

Shaping bread

When you are making rolls or baguettes, you will need to shape the dough with your hands. Make sure your hands are clean and dusted with flour to prevent sticking.

Top Tip

Yeast is a type of fungus—but don't let that put you off! It is added to dough to make it rise and become stretchy. It needs heat to activate it.

How to knead

Secure the dough with one hand at the back, then place the heel of your other hand in the middle of the dough.

Push your front hand away from you, stretching the dough with it.

With your front hand, pick up the edge of the dough and fold it back on itself. Press it into a ball. Repeat.

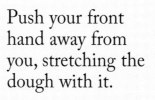

Rising

Cover the dough with a damp dish towel or oiled plastic wrap when it is rising to prevent a crust from forming. Leave it in a warm place, such as near a warm oven or in the pantry, since the yeast needs warmth to activate it. Beware—if the heat is too high, it will kill the yeast.

Basic Bread

Makes
1 loaf

Prep
1¾ hours

Cooking
30 mins

Making bread is lots of fun, and the smell of baking bread will make your mouth water! This easy basic dough recipe can be made into delicious rolls or a traditional loaf. For tips on how to knead, turn to page 43. If you want to make wholewheat bread, replace the white bread flour with wholewheat bread flour.

Ingredients

- 1½ tsp active dry yeast
- 1 tsp sugar
- 12 fl oz (350 ml) lukewarm water
- 4 cups (500 g) white bread flour
- 2 tsp salt

Bread flour

Oven mitts

Salt

Loaf pan

Tools

- 2 lb (900 g) loaf pan
- Small mixing bowl
- Wooden spoon
- Sifter
- Clean, damp dish towel
- Large mixing bowl
- Oven mitts
- Cooling rack

Large mixing bowl

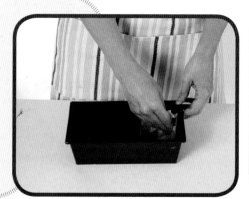

1 Lightly grease a 2 lb (900 g) loaf pan with butter. Place the yeast, sugar, and a little of the water in a small bowl, stir well, and leave in a warm place for 10 minutes, until frothy.

2 Sift the flour and salt into a large mixing bowl. Make a well in the center and pour in the frothy yeast mixture and remaining water. Stir with a wooden spoon to form a dough.

3 Knead the dough on a lightly floured surface for 10 minutes. Place back in the bowl, cover with a damp dish towel, and leave in a warm place for an hour, or until doubled in size.

  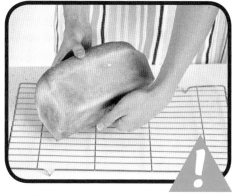

4 Preheat the oven to 425°F (220°C). Lightly "punch down" the dough to knock out the large air bubbles. Then knead it lightly on a floured surface for a few minutes.

5 Shape the dough into a rectangle and tuck the ends under to fit into the pan. Place in the pan. Cover with the damp dish towel; leave to rise in a warm place for a further 30 minutes.

6 Place the pan in the center of the oven. Bake for 30 minutes, or until risen and golden. Turn out the loaf and tap the base—it should sound hollow. Place on a cooling rack.

Variation

To make rolls: At Step 5 divide the dough into 8 balls. Flatten slightly. Place on a greased baking sheet, cover with a damp dish towel, and leave to rise for 30 minutes. Brush the tops with milk, then sprinkle over some seeds (such as sesame or sunflower). Bake for 20–25 minutes.

Scones

Medium

Makes
8–10

Prep
10 mins

Cooking
12 mins

These traditional scones, served with jam and whipped cream, will really hit the spot! The secret to making successful scones is not to handle the mixture too much or to add too much flour when rolling out the dough.

Ingredients

- 1¾ cups (225 g) self-rising flour
- 1 tsp baking powder
- Pinch of salt
- 2 oz (50 g) butter (diced)
- ¼ cup (50 g) sugar
- 5 fl oz (150 ml) milk
- Beaten egg or milk for brushing

Butter

To serve
- Whipped cream or butter, strawberry or raspberry jam

Large baking sheet

Milk

Jam

Pastry cutter

Pastry brush

Tools

- Large baking sheet
- Sifter
- Large mixing bowl
- Wooden spoon
- Round-bladed knife
- Rolling pin
- 2½" (6 cm) pastry cutter
- Pastry brush
- Oven mitts
- Cooling rack

1 Preheat the oven to 425°F (220°C). Lightly grease a large baking sheet with some butter. Sift the flour, baking powder, and salt into a large mixing bowl.

2 Using your fingertips, rub the butter into the flour mixture until the mixture resembles fine breadcrumbs. Stir in the sugar with a wooden spoon and mix together thoroughly.

3 Stir in the milk with a round-bladed knife until the mixture forms a soft dough and comes together in a ball. Gently knead the dough on a floured surface to remove any cracks.

Variation

For fruit scones, stir in ⅓ cup (50 g) raisins, golden raisins, or currants (or a mixture of these) with the sugar in Step 2 before you add the milk.

4 Roll out the dough to ¾" (2 cm) thickness, then, using a 2½" (6 cm) pastry cutter, cut into circles. Gather up any trimmings, reroll them, and cut out more scones.

5 Place the scones on a baking sheet, spacing them a little apart. Using a pastry brush, brush the tops with the egg or milk and cook for 10–12 minutes, or until risen and golden brown.

6 Transfer the scones to a cooling rack. (You can serve them warm or cold.) Cut them in half and spread with butter and jam or with whipped cream and jam.

Medium

Makes

8

Prep

10 mins

Cooking

25 mins

Cheese and Onion Round

This savory bread round makes a great accompaniment to soup or salad. It also tastes delicious on its own, spread with a little butter or low-fat spread.

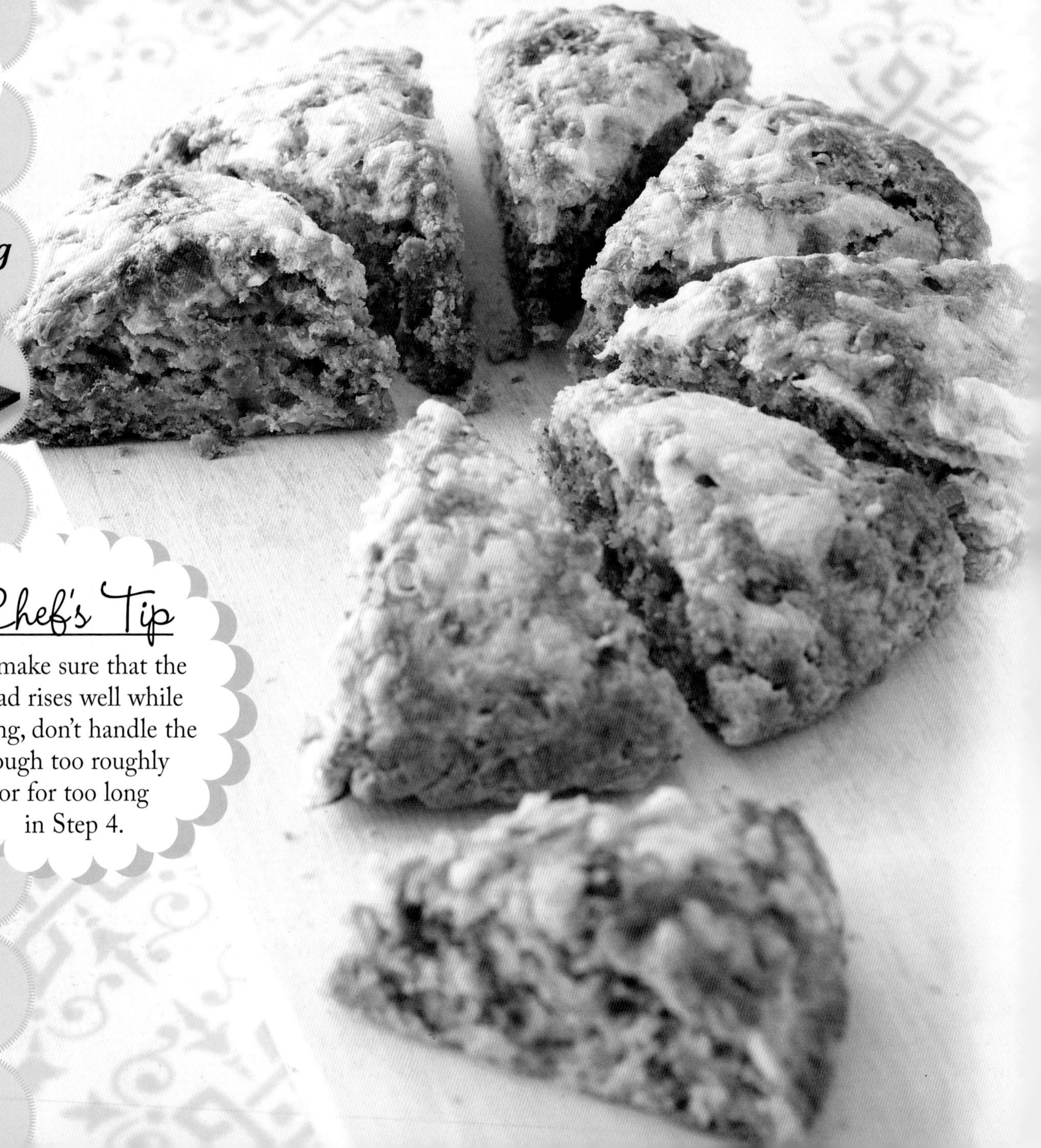

Chef's Tip

To make sure that the bread rises well while baking, don't handle the dough too roughly or for too long in Step 4.

Ingredients

Beaten egg

Cheese

- 2 oz (50 g) butter (diced)
- 1 bunch scallions, sliced (optional)
- 1 cup (125 g) self-rising flour
- 1 cup (125 g) wholewheat self-rising flour
- 1 tbsp baking powder
- ½ tsp salt
- 1 tsp mustard powder
- 1 cup (125 g) sharp Cheddar cheese (grated)
- 1 large egg
- 7 tbsp (100 ml) milk
- Beaten egg or milk (for brushing)

Scallions

Butter

Saucepan

Knife

Tools

- Baking sheet
- Saucepan
- Wooden spoon
- Large mixing bowl
- Sifter
- Round-bladed knife
- Sharp knife
- Pastry brush
- Oven mitts
- Cutting board

1 Preheat the oven to 400°F (200°C). Lightly grease a baking sheet. Melt 1 oz (25 g) of the butter in a saucepan, add the scallions, and cook over a medium heat for 2–3 minutes.

2 Sift the flours, baking powder, and salt into a bowl. Use your fingertips to rub the remaining butter into the flour, until the mixture resembles fine breadcrumbs.

3 Stir in the mustard powder, ⅔ of the cheese, and the cooked scallions, and mix well. Beat together the egg and milk, then stir them into the flour mixture with a round-bladed knife.

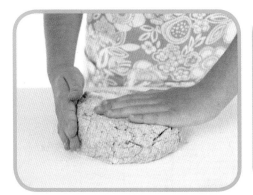

4 Gently knead the dough on a lightly floured surface to remove any cracks. Place it on the baking sheet and, using your hands, shape it into a 7" (18 cm) round about ¾" (2 cm) thick.

5 Using a sharp knife, divide the round into eight wedges, cutting deeply into the dough. Using a pastry brush, brush the tops with the egg or milk and sprinkle over the remaining cheese.

6 Cook the round for 20–25 minutes, or until risen and golden. (Cover the top with foil if it becomes too brown.) Place it on a cutting board and cut it into wedges. Serve warm or cold.

Pizza Dough

It is really easy to make your own pizza dough, and incredibly tasty! Just follow the recipe, then add tomato sauce and your favorite toppings to custom-make a delicious homemade pizza.

Makes

1

Prep

1¼ hours

Cooking

15 mins

Salt

Large mixing bowl

Rolling pin

Ingredients

- 1¾ cups (225 g) white bread flour
- ½ tsp salt
- ½ tsp fast-acting dry yeast
- 5 fl oz (150 ml) warm water
- 1 tbsp extra-virgin olive oil
- Pizza toppings of your choice

Tools

- Large mixing bowl
- Wooden spoon
- Damp dish towel
- Baking sheet
- Rolling pin
- Oven mitts

Baking sheet

Flour

Olive oil

1 Place the flour, salt, and yeast in a large mixing bowl and make a well in the center. Using a wooden spoon, stir in the warm water and olive oil to form a dough.

2 Place the dough on a lightly floured surface and knead for 7–10 minutes until it is smooth and elastic. (For tips on how to knead, turn to page 43.)

3 Place the dough in a lightly oiled bowl, cover with a clean damp dish towel, and leave to rise in a warm place for an hour, or until the dough has doubled in size.

Variation

To give your pizza an herby zing, try adding a tablespoon of dried oregano in Step 1.

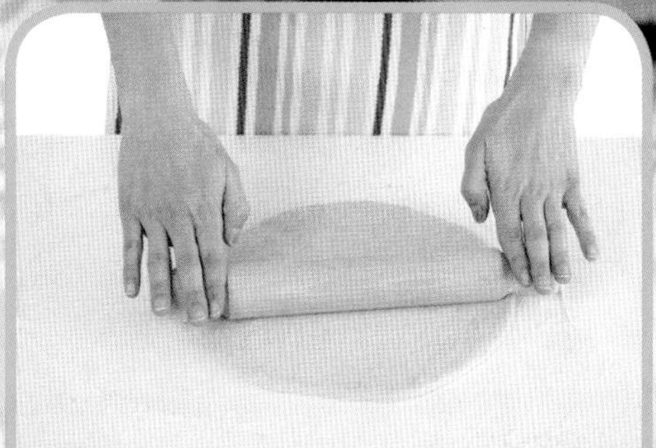

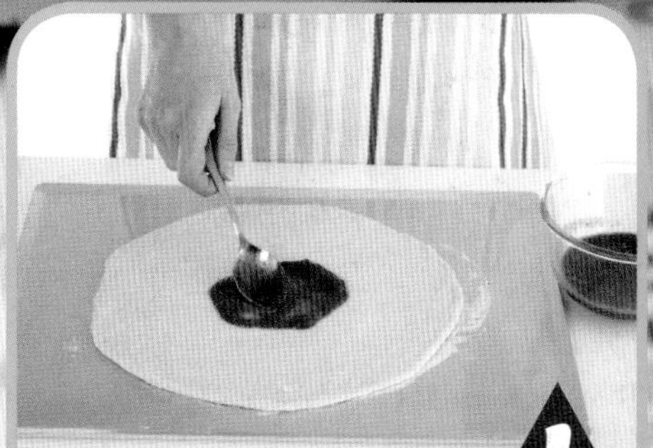

4 Preheat the oven to 425°F (220°C). Lightly oil a baking sheet with some olive oil. "Punch down" the risen dough to get rid of the air bubbles.

5 Knead the dough on a lightly floured surface for 2–3 minutes. Then, using a lightly floured rolling pin, roll out the dough to a 12" (30 cm) circle.

6 Place the pizza base on the baking sheet, then add the toppings of your choice. Bake for 10–15 minutes on the top rack of the oven until the dough is crisp and the toppings have cooked.

Multigrain Braid

This multigrain braid is fun to make and nutritious. If you want to make a white-bread braid, just substitute white bread flour for the multigrain bread flour.

Makes
1
loaf

Prep
15
mins

Cooking
30
mins

1 Place the yeast, sugar, and a little of the water in a small bowl. Stir well with a teaspoon and leave in a warm place for 10 minutes, until the mixture turns frothy.

2 Place the flour and salt in a large mixing bowl. Then rub in the butter with your fingertips until it is thoroughly mixed into the multigrain flour.

3 Make a well in the center and pour in the frothy yeast mixture and remaining water. Stir with a wooden spoon to form a dough, then use your hands to form a ball.

Ingredients

- 1½ tsp active dry yeast
- 1 tsp sugar
- 12 fl oz (350 ml) lukewarm water
- 4 cups (500 g) multigrain bread flour
- 2 tsp salt
- 1 oz (25 g) butter (diced)
- Extra flour for dusting

Sugar

Flour

Large mixing bowl

Butter

Salt

Tools

- Small mixing bowl
- Teaspoon
- Large mixing bowl
- Wooden spoon
- Clean, damp dish towel
- Baking sheet
- Knife
- Oven mitts

Wooden spoon

Baking sheet

4 Knead the dough on a lightly floured surface for 10 minutes until the dough is smooth and elastic. (See page 43 for tips on how to knead dough.)

5 Place the dough in a lightly oiled bowl, cover with a clean, damp dish towel, and leave to rise in a warm place for an hour, or until it has doubled in size.

6 Preheat the oven to 425°F (220°C). Lightly grease a baking sheet. Place the dough on a lightly floured surface. Lightly "punch down" the dough to get rid of the air bubbles.

7 Shape the dough into a rectangle, then cut it into three equal pieces. Use your hands to roll each piece of dough into a 12" (30 cm) long sausage.

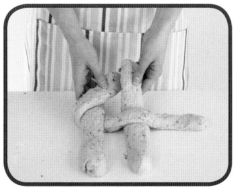

8 Make an "H" with the dough pieces, weaving the middle piece over the piece on the left and under the piece on the right. Braid from the center downward. Turn the dough around and repeat.

9 Tuck the ends under and place on the baking sheet. Leave to rise for a further 30 minutes. Bake for 30 minutes, or until hollow when tapped. Remove from the pan and leave to cool.

Sticky Fruit Buns

Makes
10

Prep
2½ hours

Cooking
30 mins

These sweet, fruity buns are made with honey for extra stickiness! This fruit bun recipe calls for pumpkin pie spice, but you can leave this out if you prefer.

1 Place the flour, yeast, and sugar in a large mixing bowl. Make a well in the center of the mixture and crack the egg into the well. (To crack the egg, just tap it on the rim of the bowl.)

2 Melt the butter in a saucepan over a low heat, then add the milk and warm through. Add this to the large bowl and mix together with a round-bladed knife.

3 Turn the dough onto a lightly floured surface and knead for 10 minutes. Return to the bowl, cover with a clean, damp dish towel, and leave in a warm place for about 1½ hours.

Honey

Ingredients

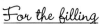
Raisins

- 3 cups (350 g) white bread flour
- 1 package (¼ oz/7 g) fast-acting dry yeast
- 2 tbsp (25 g) sugar
- 1 large egg
- 3½ oz (100 g) butter (diced)
- 6 fl oz (175 ml) milk

Brown sugar

For the filling

- 1 oz (25 g) butter (diced)
- 1 cup (150 g) mixed raisins, currants, and golden raisins
- 4 tbsp (25 g) mixed peel (candied citrus peel)
- ¼ cup (50 g) brown sugar
- 1 tsp pumpkin pie spice (optional)
- Grated zest of 1 lemon
- 1 tbsp honey

Tools

- Two large mixing bowls
- Saucepan
- Round-bladed knife
- Clean, damp dish towel
- 9" (23 cm) round shallow cake pan
- Parchment paper
- Rolling pin
- Pastry brush
- Spoon
- Sharp knife
- Oven mitts
- Aluminum foil
- Cooling rack

Knife

Oven mitts

Wooden spoon

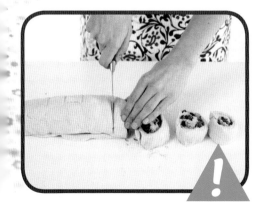

4 Grease the bottom and sides of a 9" (23 cm) round, shallow cake pan and line the bottom with parchment paper so that the buns don't stick in the pan. Preheat the oven to 400°F (200°C).

5 "Punch down" the dough, then place it on a floured surface. Roll the dough out into a 14" (30 cm) square. Brush the melted butter all over the dough, using a pastry brush.

6 Mix together the dried fruit, mixed peel, brown sugar, pumpkin pie spice, and lemon zest. Sprinkle on top of the pastry, leaving a ½" (1 cm) border. Roll the dough into a sausage shape.

7 Use a sharp knife to cut the dough into 10 pieces. Place them with their cut sides face up in the pan. Cover them with the clean, damp dish towel and leave in a warm place for 35–40 minutes.

8 Bake the buns on the top rack of the oven for about 25–30 minutes, until golden. If they start to become too brown, cover them with aluminum foil until baked.

9 Carefully brush the buns with the honey, taking care not to burn yourself on the hot pan. Leave the buns to cool in the pan for 3–4 minutes. Then place them on a cooling rack.

55

Italian Bread

This dimpled bread is known as focaccia and can be flavored with herbs, cheese, sun-dried tomatoes, or olives. It's so yummy, you'll keep coming back for more!

Serves

6–8

Prep

2 hours

Cooking

25 mins

Variation

For rosemary focaccia, mix 2 tbsp (30 ml) chopped fresh rosemary into the dough at Step 2. Add 1 cup (100 g) of freshly grated Parmesan in Step 2 for cheese focaccia.

1 Sift the flour into a large mixing bowl, add the salt, and stir in the yeast with a large metal spoon. Lightly oil a baking sheet to prevent the focaccia from sticking.

2 Make a well in the center of the flour with the large metal spoon. Stir in the warm water and olive oil until the mixture starts to come together to form a smooth dough.

Ingredients

- 3 cups (350 g) white bread flour
- 1 package (¼ oz/7 g) fast-acting dry yeast
- ½ tsp salt
- 6 fl oz (175 ml) warm water
- 2 fl oz (50 ml) olive oil

To finish
- 1 tbsp olive oil
- Coarse sea salt for sprinkling

Bread flour

Salt

Olive oil

Baking sheet

Sifter

Tools

- Sifter
- Large mixing bowl
- Large metal spoon
- Baking sheet
- Clean, damp dish towel
- Rolling pin
- Oven mitts

Rolling pin

Variation

For sun-dried tomato or olive focaccia, stir in ⅓ cup (50 g) olives or sun-dried tomatoes in oil, (drained and roughly chopped) at Step 2.

3 Transfer to a lightly floured surface and knead for 10 minutes until smooth and elastic. Return to the bowl, cover with a clean, damp dish towel, and leave to rise in a warm place for an hour.

4 "Punch down" the dough to remove the large air bubbles, then place on a lightly floured surface. Using a rolling pin, roll out to an 8" (20 cm) circle just over ½ in (1 cm) thick.

5 Place the rolled-out dough on the oiled baking sheet and cover with a clean, damp dish towel. Leave the dough to rise in a warm place for 30 minutes.

6 Preheat the oven to 400°F (200°C). Using your fingertips, make dimples all over the surface of the risen dough and drizzle with the olive oil.

7 Sprinkle the dough with the sea salt. Place in the oven on the middle rack. Bake for 20–25 minutes until risen and golden. It's delicious when eaten warm!

Easy

Cornbread

Makes
24

This cornbread recipe is really simple to make, and the corn and scallions give it an unusual chunky, yet light, texture.

Prep
10
mins

Cooking
30
mins

Variation

If you want to heat things up, try chili cornbread! Simply add 1 finely chopped fresh red chili in Step 2.

Chef's Tip

This cornbread makes a filling accompaniment to soup or salad. It also tastes great on its own!

Ingredients

- 1 cup (125 g) all-purpose flour
- 4 oz (125 g) cornmeal or polenta
- 1 tbsp baking powder
- 1 tsp salt
- 5 scallions, thinly chopped (optional)
- 1 cup (150 g) canned corn

- 2 medium eggs
- 1¼ cups (285 ml) buttermilk or natural yogurt
- 7 tbsp (100 ml) milk
- 2 oz (50 g) butter (melted and cooled)

Eggs

Polenta

Salt

Scallions

Buttermilk

Measuring cup

Tools

- 8" (20 cm) square cake pan
- Parchment paper
- Large mixing bowl
- Wooden spoon
- Measuring cup
- Whisk
- Oven mitts
- Sharp knife

Large mixing bowl

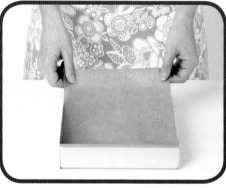

1 Grease an 8" (20 cm) square cake pan and then line the bottom with parchment paper to prevent the cornbread from sticking. Preheat the oven to 400°F (200°C).

2 In a large mixing bowl, place the flour, cornmeal or polenta, baking powder, salt, chopped scallions, and corn. Mix together thoroughly with a wooden spoon.

3 In a measuring cup, whisk together the eggs, buttermilk (or yogurt), milk, and melted butter with a small whisk until they are thoroughly combined and frothy.

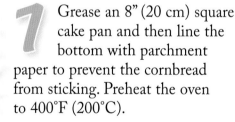

4 Pour the egg and milk mixture into the flour mixture in the large mixing bowl. Stir with a wooden spoon to combine all the ingredients thoroughly.

5 Pour the mixture into the prepared pan. Bake for 25–30 minutes until golden brown and beginning to pull away from the sides of the pan. Allow to cool in the pan before cutting into squares.

Variation

For an extra indulgent treat, try topping the cornbread with a little grated cheese before baking.

Flatbreads

These flatbreads taste great served with hummus and dips, or with barbecued food. They are best eaten as soon as they are cooked, when they are still soft and warm.

Makes

6

Prep

1¼ hours

Cooking

3 mins

Variation

Try adding different ingredients to the flour mixture in Step 1, such as 1 tbsp of freshly chopped rosemary, chopped scallions, or crushed garlic.

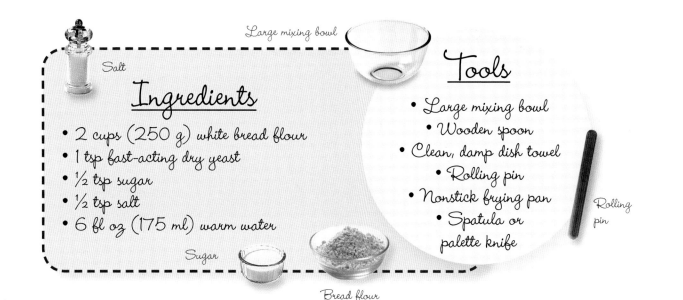

Ingredients

- 2 cups (250 g) white bread flour
- 1 tsp fast-acting dry yeast
- ½ tsp sugar
- ½ tsp salt
- 6 fl oz (175 ml) warm water

Salt

Sugar

Bread flour

Tools

- Large mixing bowl
- Wooden spoon
- Clean, damp dish towel
- Rolling pin
- Nonstick frying pan
- Spatula or palette knife

Large mixing bowl

Rolling pin

1 Place the flour, yeast, sugar, and salt in a large mixing bowl and mix well with a wooden spoon. Make a well in the center and stir in enough of the water to form a soft dough.

2 Place the dough on a lightly floured surface and knead for 5 minutes until smooth and elastic. (If you need tips on how to knead, turn to page 43.)

3 Return the dough to the bowl and cover with a clean, damp dish towel. Leave it in a warm place for an hour or until the dough has doubled in size.

4 "Punch down" the dough with your fist to remove the large air bubbles, then divide the dough into six equal chunks with your hands.

5 Knead each chunk lightly, on a lightly floured surface, to make a flatter, round shape. Then roll out each piece of dough into a 5" (13 cm) diameter circle with a rolling pin.

6 Preheat a frying pan. Add a flat piece of dough and cook for a minute, until golden underneath. Then flip it over and cook the other side for 30 seconds. Serve immediately.

61

Cakes

Cakes may look complicated, but they are usually very simple to make. Preparation is the key, so make sure you understand the basic techniques and your cakes will turn out just right.

Top Tip

To ensure your cake bakes successfully, it is important to use the right size cake pans, as stated in the recipe.

Creaming

Mixing together sugar and butter is called creaming. If your butter is at room temperature you will find it much easier to mix than if it's cold.

Correct temperature

It is very important to use your ingredients at the correct temperature. Eggs should be at room temperature, otherwise they might curdle.

Testing a cake with a skewer

To test whether a cake is cooked properly, stick a skewer or knife in it. It will come out clean if the cake is baked. If it has cake mixture on it, put the cake back in the oven for 5 minutes.

Top Tip

Do not be tempted to open the oven door while your cake is baking—a sudden gush of cold air might make it sink in the middle! Wait until the cooking time is nearly finished before checking.

How to line a cake pan

1. Put the cake pan on top of some parchment paper and draw around the bottom with a pencil or pen.

2. Cut out the shape with scissors and place the parchment paper inside the pan.

Folding

Folding is a gentle method of mixing that keeps a cake light and airy. Use a metal spoon to fold the mixture over itself, instead of stirring it in a circle.

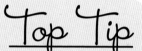

Simple Sponge Cake

Serves

6–8

Prep

10 mins

Cooking

30 mins

This cake is wonderfully light and moist. You can also make individual cupcakes with this recipe (turn to page 122 for tips on decoration).

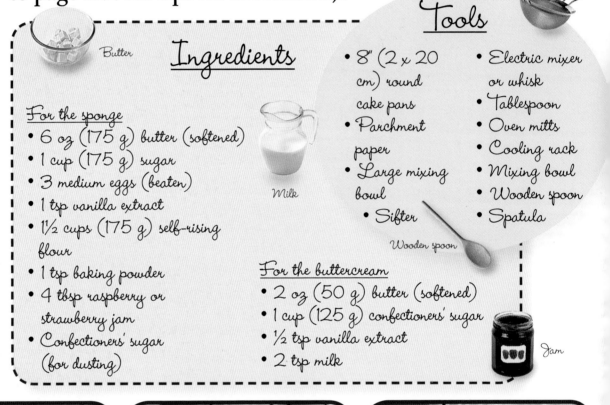

Butter

Milk

Wooden spoon

Jam

Sifter

Ingredients

For the sponge
- 6 oz (175 g) butter (softened)
- 1 cup (175 g) sugar
- 3 medium eggs (beaten)
- 1 tsp vanilla extract
- 1½ cups (175 g) self-rising flour
- 1 tsp baking powder
- 4 tbsp raspberry or strawberry jam
- Confectioners' sugar (for dusting)

For the buttercream
- 2 oz (50 g) butter (softened)
- 1 cup (125 g) confectioners' sugar
- ½ tsp vanilla extract
- 2 tsp milk

Tools
- 8" (2 x 20 cm) round cake pans
- Parchment paper
- Large mixing bowl
- Sifter
- Electric mixer or whisk
- Tablespoon
- Oven mitts
- Cooling rack
- Mixing bowl
- Wooden spoon
- Spatula

1 Preheat the oven to 350°F (180°C). Grease two 8" (20 cm) round cake pans and line each with parchment paper so that the sponge cakes don't stick.

2 Place the butter, sugar, eggs, and vanilla extract in a large bowl and sift over the flour and baking powder. Using an electric mixer or whisk, beat all the ingredients together until thick.

3 Divide the mixture between the two pans, leveling the tops with the back of a tablespoon. Bake in the center of the oven for 25–30 minutes, or until risen and firm to the touch.

4 Leave the cakes to cool in the pans for a few minutes, then turn them out onto a cooling rack. Peel off the parchment paper and allow the cakes to cool completely.

5 To make the buttercream filling, place the butter, confectioners' sugar, vanilla extract, and milk in a mixing bowl. Beat them together with a wooden spoon until smooth and creamy.

6 Spread the flat side of one of the cakes with the jam. Spread the flat side of the other with the buttercream, then sandwich the two halves together. Dust with confectioners' sugar.

Variation

This mixture will also make 20 cupcakes. Simply divide the mixture between paper baking cups and bake for 15 minutes.

Hard

Serves
12

Prep
35 mins

Cooking
30 mins

Double Chocolate Fudge Cake

If you are a chocolate lover, you will adore this cake! The dark chocolate sponge is filled and topped with a white chocolate icing.

Tools

Cake pans

- 2 x 8" (20 cm) cake pans
- Parchment paper
- Two large mixing bowls
- Electric mixer or whisk
- Sifter
- Spatula
- Oven mitts
- Cooling rack
- Heat-proof bowl
- Saucepan
- Wooden spoon
- Palette knife

Sifter

Eggs

Ingredients

For the cake
- 6 oz (175 g) butter (softened)
- 1¼ cups (175 g) brown sugar
- 1¼ cups (150 g) self-rising flour
- ¼ cup (25 g) cocoa powder
- 1 tbsp baking powder
- ½ tsp baking soda
- 3 medium eggs (beaten)
- ½ cup (100 ml) sour cream

For the icing
- 6 oz (175 g) white chocolate (broken into small pieces)
- 4 oz (125 g) butter
- 4 tbsp milk
- 1¾ cups (200 g) confectioners' sugar

Milk

To decorate: Grated chocolate, chocolate buttons, and cocoa powder for dusting (optional)

Brown sugar

1 Preheat the oven to 325°F (170°C). Grease and line the bottoms of the pans with parchment paper. Place the butter and sugar in a mixing bowl and mix together until combined.

2 Sift in the flour, cocoa powder, baking powder, and baking soda. Add the eggs and the sour cream and beat with an electric mixer or whisk until combined.

3 Divide the mixture between the two pans and level the tops. Bake for 25–30 minutes. Leave to cool slightly, then turn out onto a cooling rack. Remove the parchment paper.

4 To make the icing, place the chocolate, butter, and milk in a heat-proof bowl over a saucepan of simmering water. Stir occasionally until the ingredients are melted and smooth.

5 Sift the confectioners' sugar into a bowl, then pour over the melted chocolate mixture. Beat together with the mixer or whisk. Allow the icing to cool, then beat again until it forms soft peaks.

6 Use a little of the icing to sandwich the two cakes together. Spread the remaining icing over the top and sides of the cake. Decorate as desired and dust with cocoa powder.

Carrot Cupcakes

Medium

Makes 18

Prep 10 mins

Cooking 20 mins

The grated carrots make these little cupcakes perfectly moist, and the yummy cream-cheese frosting adds a deliciously tangy topping.

Butter

Carrots

Tools

- Muffin pan
- 18 paper baking cups
- Large mixing bowl
- Electric mixer or whisk
- Sifter
- Dessert spoon
- Oven mitts
- Cooling rack
- Wooden spoon
- Medium bowl

Muffin pan

Electric mixer

Ingredients

- 6 oz (175 g) butter (softened)
- 1 cup (175 g) sugar
- 1½ cup (175 g) self-rising flour
- 2 tsp pumpkin pie spice
- 2 large eggs
- Grated zest of 1 orange and 1 tbsp juice
- 2 medium carrots (peeled and coarsely grated)
- ½ cup (50 g) walnuts, toasted and chopped (optional)

Frosting

- 7 oz (200 g) cream cheese
- 2 tbsp confectioners' sugar
- 1 tbsp orange juice
- 2 tsp grated orange zest

Orange

Orange juice

1 Preheat the oven to 350°F (180°C). Place 18 paper baking cups in a muffin pan. Most muffin pans have only 12 holes so you may have to use two pans or cook in batches.

2 In a large mixing bowl, beat together the butter and sugar until they become pale and fluffy. Use an electric mixer if you have one. If not, then use a whisk.

3 Sift the flour and pumpkin pie spice into the bowl. Then add the eggs, orange juice, and zest. Beat until all the ingredients are completely combined.

68

4 Stir the grated carrots and nuts (if you are using them) into the mixing bowl. Divide the mixture equally between the 18 baking cups using a dessert spoon.

5 Bake for 18–20 minutes in the middle of the oven until risen and golden brown. Remove from the oven using the oven mitts and place on a cooling rack to cool completely.

6 Beat together all the frosting ingredients with a wooden spoon. Spread the frosting over the cooled cupcakes and decorate the cupcakes with extra orange zest.

Banana and Buttermilk Loaf

This loaf has a wonderful crumbly texture, combined with crunchy nuts and soft gooey banana. It is a great way to use up any ripe bananas.

Variation

Replace the pecans with chopped walnuts or brazil nuts, or just leave them out.

Ingredients

Bananas

Butter

- 3 ripe bananas (broken into pieces)
- 1 tsp lemon juice
- 1 cup (100 g) pecan nut halves (optional)
- 3½ oz (100 g) butter (softened)
- 1¼ cups (175 g) brown sugar
- 2 medium eggs (beaten)
- 1 tsp vanilla extract

- 2 cups (250 g) all-purpose flour
- 1 tsp salt
- 1 tsp baking soda
- 1 tsp pumpkin pie spice
- 4 fl oz (100 ml) buttermilk

For the topping
- 1 small banana (sliced)

Lemon juice

Electric mixer

Tools

Loaf pan

- 2 lb (900 g) loaf pan
- Parchment paper
- Two small bowls
- Fork
- Large mixing bowl
- Electric mixer or whisk
- Sifter
- Metal spoon
- Oven mitts
- Aluminum foil
- Cooling rack

1 Preheat the oven to 350°F (180°C). Grease and line the bottom of a 2 lb (900 g) loaf pan with parchment paper. Mash the banana pieces with the lemon juice, using a fork.

2 Use your hands to break the pecan halves into small pieces into a bowl, if you are adding nuts. If you don't like nuts, just leave this step out.

3 Place the butter and sugar in a large mixing bowl. Using an electric mixer or whisk, beat them together until they are combined and become light and fluffy.

4 Beat in the eggs and vanilla extract, a little at a time. Stir in the banana mixture. Sift in the flour, salt, baking soda, and pumpkin pie spice and stir into the mixture with a metal spoon.

5 Mix in the buttermilk. Stir in the nuts if you are using them, saving a few. Pour the mixture into the pan and place the sliced banana on the top. Sprinkle the saved nuts over the top.

6 Bake in the oven for 50–60 minutes. If the loaf becomes too brown, cover it with foil. Allow the loaf to cool in the pan, then place it on a cooling rack and remove the parchment paper.

Marble Cake

Chocolate and orange cake mixtures are swirled together to make this spectacular marble-effect cake. This cake is lots of fun to make and you can change your swirling patterns every time you make it! Serve it cold or hot, with custard or whipped cream. Delicious!

Serves

25

Prep

10 mins

Cooking

30 mins

Orange

Butter

Tools

Electric mixer

Ingredients

- 6 oz (175 g) butter (softened)
- 1 cup (175 g) sugar
- 1½ cups (175 g) self-rising flour
- 3 large eggs
- Grated zest of 1 orange
- 2 tbsp orange juice
- 2 tbsp cocoa powder

- 8" (20 cm) square cake pan
- Parchment paper
- Large mixing bowl
- Electric mixer or whisk
- Large spoon
- Sifter
- Round-bladed knife
- Oven mitts
- Cutting board
- Sharp knife

Sugar

Eggs

Square cake pan

1 Preheat the oven to 350°F (180°C). Grease and line the bottom of an 8" (20 cm) square cake pan with parchment paper to prevent the cake from sticking.

2 Place all the ingredients except the cocoa powder in a large mixing bowl. Using an electric mixer or whisk, beat them all together until mixed and smooth.

3 Divide the mixture in half. Place large spoonfuls of one half of the mixture into the pan in each of the four corners and in the middle. Leave space between each spoonful.

Variation

Experiment by flavoring the cake with a teaspoon of vanilla or peppermint extract instead of orange.

4 Sift the cocoa powder over the remaining mixture in the bowl and mix together until combined. Spoon the chocolate mixture into the spaces in the cake pan.

5 Gently drag a round-bladed knife through the mixtures to create a swirl effect with the brown and white mixtures. Don't overdo it, or you will mix the two colors together completely.

6 Bake the cake for 30 minutes, until well risen and springy. Allow it to cool in the pan, then remove it, and peel off the parchment paper. Cut it into 25 squares with a sharp knife.

Medium

Serves
8

Prep
20 mins

Cooking
40 mins

Lemon Drizzle Cake

It would be hard to find a more lemony cake than this one. This luscious lemon sponge cake has a contrasting crusty top made by pouring the lemon syrup over the cake while it is still warm.

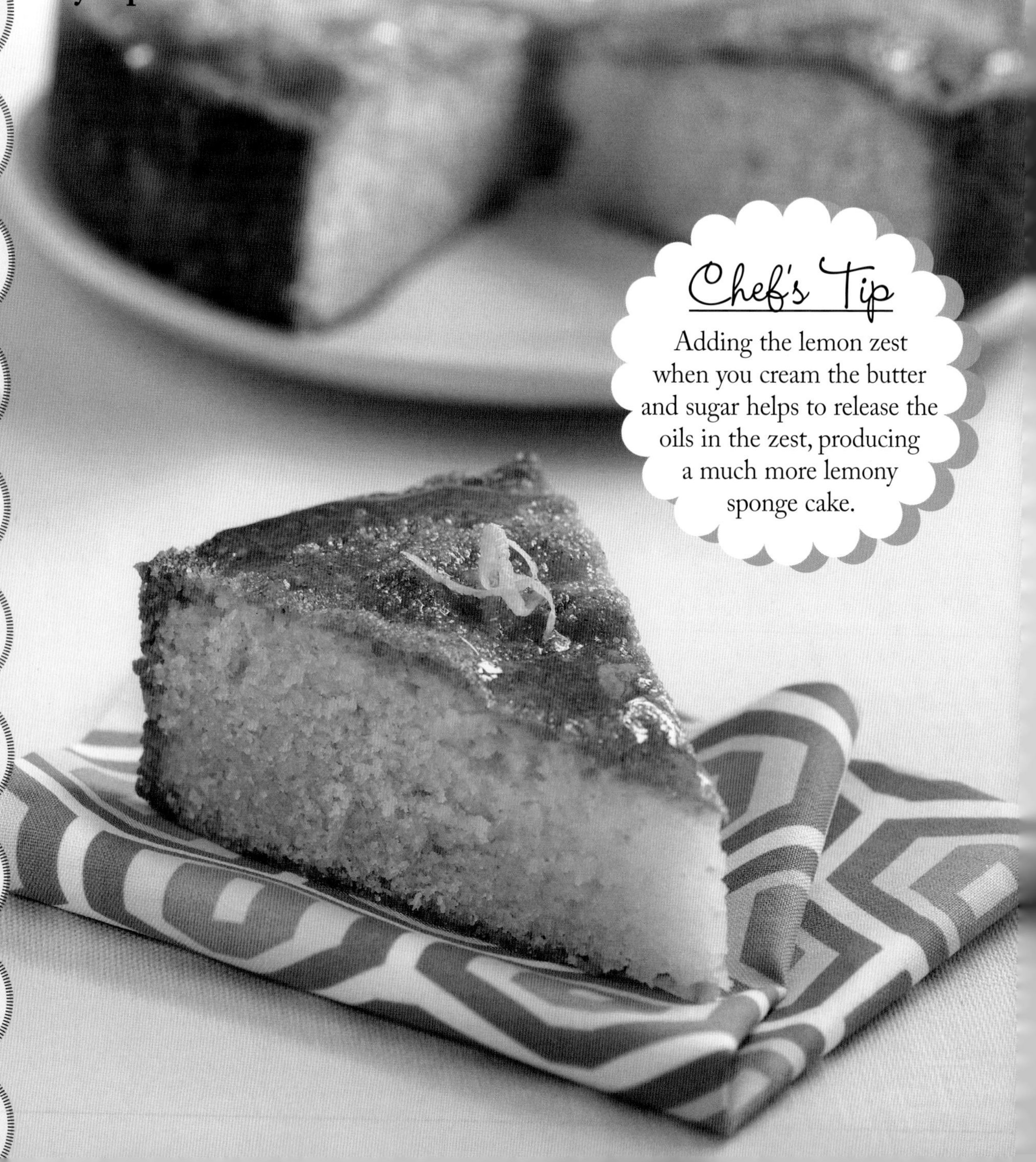

Chef's Tip

Adding the lemon zest when you cream the butter and sugar helps to release the oils in the zest, producing a much more lemony sponge cake.

Ingredients

Sugar

Flour

Lemon sponge
- Finely grated zest of 2 unwaxed lemons
- 7 oz (200 g) butter (softened)
- 1 cup (200 g) sugar
- 3 medium eggs (beaten)
- 1²/₃ cups (200 g) self-rising flour (sifted)

Syrup
- Juice of 4 lemons (about 3½ fl oz/100 ml)
- ⅓ cup (75 g) sugar

Lemons

Unsalted butter

Eggs

Large mixing bowl

Tools

- 8" (20 cm) round springform cake pan
- Parchment paper
- Large mixing bowl
- Electric mixer or whisk
- Metal spoon
- Oven mitts
- Small mixing bowl
- Toothpick
- Cooling rack

1 Preheat the oven to 350°F (180°C). Butter an 8" (20 cm) round, spring-form cake pan and line the bottom with parchment paper to prevent the cake from sticking to the pan.

2 Place the lemon zest, butter, and sugar in a large mixing bowl and beat until the mixture is light and fluffy. You can use an electric mixer or a whisk.

3 Whisk in the eggs a little at a time. If the mixture starts to curdle, add 1 tbsp of the flour. Use a metal spoon to fold in the flour, then spoon the mixture into the prepared pan.

4 Bake the cake in the center of the oven for 35–40 minutes. Put the lemon juice and sugar in a small bowl. Leave in a warm place, stirring occasionally.

5 When the cake has risen, and is golden and shrinking from the pan, remove it from the oven and prick all over with a toothpick about 20 times.

6 Drizzle the lemon juice over the cake slowly. It will leave a crust as it sinks in. Allow the cake to cool in the pan for 10 minutes, then carefully transfer it to a cooling rack.

Savory Muffins

Cheese and zucchini give these savory muffins a yummy flavor. They are perfect for a midmorning snack or you can pack one to take in your lunch!

Makes

12

Prep

10 mins

Cooking

25 mins

Variation

To make spinach and cheese muffins, replace the grated zucchini with 6 cups (180 g) chopped baby spinach leaves in Step 3.

Ingredients

- 2 medium-sized zucchinis
- 4 oz (125 g) sharp, hard cheese (such as Cheddar)
- 2¼ cups (275 g) all-purpose flour
- 1 tbsp baking powder
- 1 tbsp sugar

- 1 tsp salt
- ½ tsp ground black pepper
- 2 medium eggs (beaten)
- 6 fl oz (175 ml) milk
- 3 oz (85 g) lightly salted butter (melted)

Milk

All-purpose flour

Sifter

Cheese

Muffin pan

Tools

- 2 x 6-hole or a 12-hole muffin pan
- 12 paper baking cups
- Cheese grater
- Large mixing bowl
- Sifter
- Metal spoon
- Pitcher
- Fork or whisk
- Oven mitts
- Cooling rack

1 Preheat the oven to 375°F (190°C). Line a muffin pan with 12 paper baking cups. Trim the ends off the zucchinis and grate them coarsely. Then grate the cheese.

2 In a large mixing bowl, sift together the flour and the baking powder. Stir in the sugar, salt, and pepper with a metal spoon until they are thoroughly mixed together.

3 Add most of the grated cheese (but save a little to sprinkle over the top) and grated zucchini. Using the metal spoon, mix well to combine all the ingredients.

4 In a pitcher, beat together the eggs, milk, and butter with a fork or whisk. Pour them into the large mixing bowl and stir until just combined. The batter should be lumpy.

5 Using the metal spoon, divide the mixture equally between the 12 baking cups and sprinkle each one with the remaining grated cheese.

6 Place the muffins in the center of the oven and bake for 20–25 minutes until risen, golden, and firm. Leave to cool on a cooling rack before serving them warm or cold.

Blueberry and Sour Cream Cake

Adding sour cream makes this pretty cake wonderfully moist and creamy. It can be decorated with fresh blueberries for an extra burst of fruity flavor!

Variation

Fresh raspberries will also work in this recipe. Replace the blueberries in Steps 4 and 6 with the same amount of raspberries.

Ingredients

Lemon

Sour cream

For the cake

- 3 oz (75 g) butter (softened)
- 1¼ cup (250 g) sugar
- 1¼ cup (285 ml) sour cream
- 2 medium eggs
- 2 tsp vanilla extract
- 2½ cups (300 g) self-rising flour
- 1 tsp baking powder
- 1½ cups (225 g) blueberries

For the frosting

- 7 oz (200 g) cream cheese
- Finely grated zest of 1 lemon
- 1 tsp vanilla extract
- 1 tbsp lemon juice
- 1 cup (100 g) confectioners' sugar (sifted)
- ¾ cup (125 g) blueberries

Butter

Blueberries

Large mixing bowl

Tools

Metal spoon

Cake pan

- 9" (23 cm) round springform cake pan
- Parchment paper
- Two large mixing bowls
- Electric mixer or whisk
- Sifter
- Metal spoon
- Cooling rack
- Small bowl
- Wooden spoon
- Oven mitts
- Palette knife

1 Preheat the oven to 350°F (180°C). Grease a 9" (23 cm) round springform cake pan and line the bottom with parchment paper to prevent the cake from sticking.

2 Place the butter and sugar in a large mixing bowl. Using an electric mixer or whisk, cream the butter and sugar together until they are light and fluffy.

3 Beat in a little of the sour cream until the mixture is smooth. Then beat in the remaining sour cream, eggs, and vanilla extract until thoroughly combined and smooth.

4 Sift the flour and baking powder over the mixture and gently fold together using a metal spoon. Gently fold in the blueberries, then spoon the mixture into the pan. Level the top.

5 Bake for 45–50 minutes, or until the cake feels firm. Leave the cake to cool in the pan for 10 minutes, then place it on a cooling rack and peel off the paper. Leave to cool completely.

6 Mix the cream cheese, lemon zest, and juice with a wooden spoon in a bowl. Sift the confectioners' sugar over the mixture and beat in. Spread the frosting on the cake; decorate with blueberries.

Cake Roll

Deliciously light sponge cake is combined with fruity jam in this classic dessert. The technique can be tricky to master, so you might need to ask an adult to help you.

Serves
8

Prep
15 mins

Cooking
10 mins

Variation

For a chocolate cake roll, replace ¼ cup (25 g) of the flour with cocoa powder. This variation is delicious filled with chocolate buttercream icing (see page 122).

1 Preheat the oven to 400°F (200°C). Brush the base and sides of a 13" x 9" (33 cm x 23 cm) pan with vegetable oil, then line with parchment paper. Brush with a little more oil.

2 Beat the eggs and sugar together in a bowl, using an electric mixer. Beat for about 10 minutes until the mixture is light and frothy and the beaters leave a trail when lifted.

Ingredients

- 1 tbsp vegetable oil
- 3 large eggs
- ⅔ cup (125 g) sugar, plus extra
- 1 cup (125 g) self-rising flour

For the filling

- 5 tbsp raspberry jam

Sugar

Eggs

Vegetable oil

Jam

Tools

Knife

- 13" x 9" (33 cm x 23 cm) pan
- Pastry brush
- Parchment paper
- Large mixing bowl
- Electric mixer
- Sifter
- Metal spoon
- Oven mitts
- Clean, damp dish towel
- Sharp knife
- Palette knife

Electric mixer

3 Sift the flour into the mixture, carefully folding at the same time with a metal spoon. Pour the mixture into the prepared pan and shake it gently so that the mixture is level.

4 Place the filled pan on the top shelf of the oven. Bake for about 10 minutes, or until the sponge cake is a golden brown and begins to shrink from the edges of the pan.

5 Lay out a clean, damp dish towel on the work surface. Place a piece of parchment paper a little bigger than the size of the pan onto the dish towel and sprinkle it with sugar.

6 Using oven mitts, transfer the warm cake onto the sugared paper so that it is upside down. Take off the oven mitts and gently loosen the parchment paper and peel it off.

7 Trim the edges of the sponge cake with a knife. Make a score mark 1" (2.5 cm) from one shorter edge, being careful not to cut right through. This makes the cake easier to roll.

8 Leave the sponge cake to cool slightly, then spread with jam, using a palette knife. Roll up the cake firmly from the cut end. Place the cake on a plate seam-side down and serve in slices.

Medium

Makes

10

Prep

10 mins

Cooking

25 mins

Orange and Poppy Seed Muffins

These scrumptious muffins have a zingy, fresh orange taste and the poppy seeds add a slight crunch to the texture.

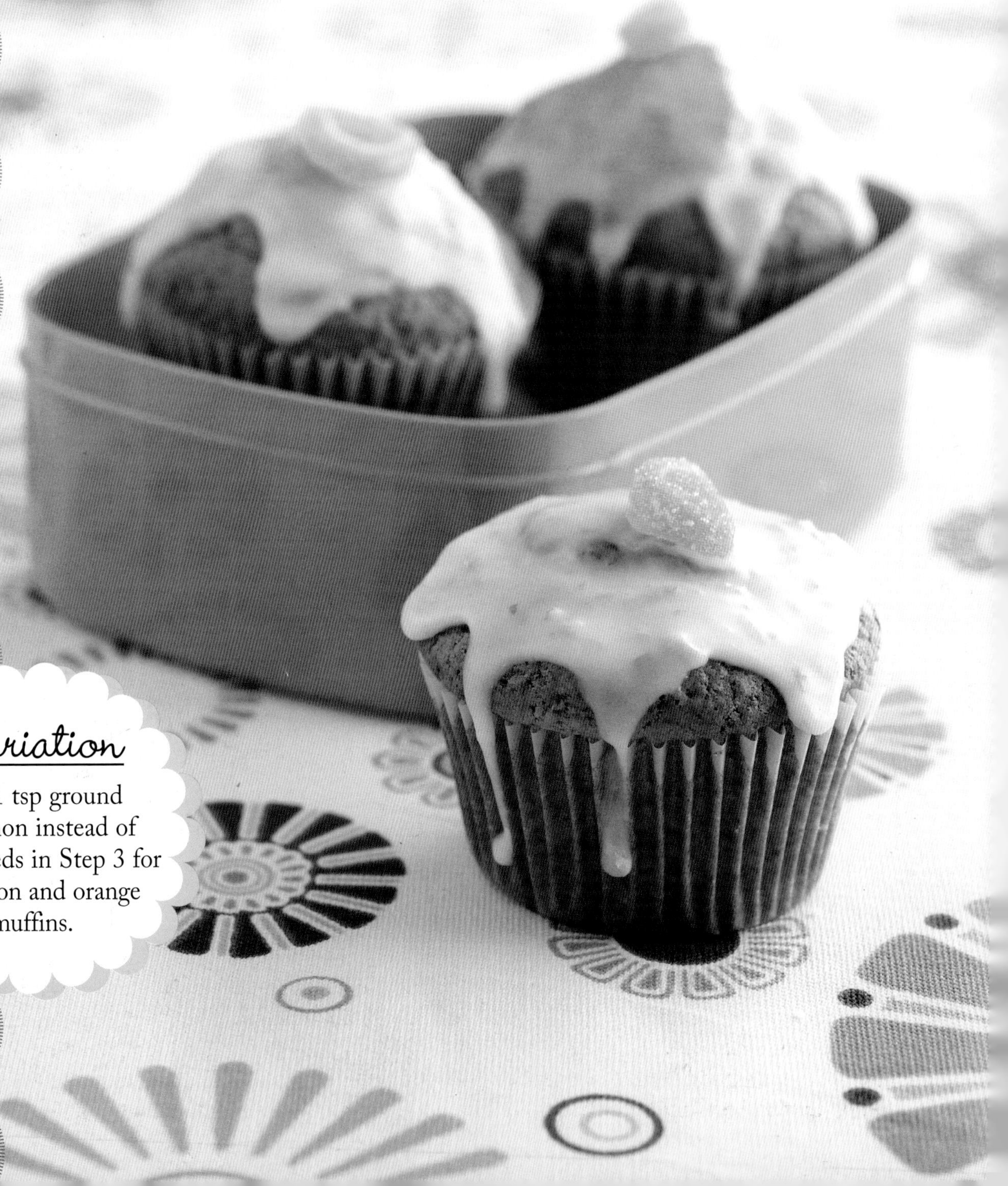

Variation

Add 1 tsp ground cinnamon instead of poppy seeds in Step 3 for cinnamon and orange muffins.

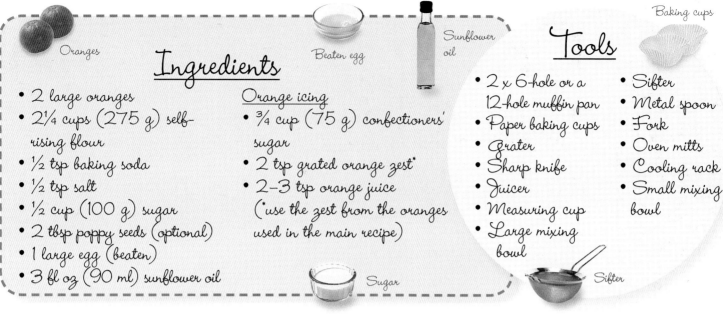

Ingredients

- 2 large oranges
- 2¼ cups (275 g) self-rising flour
- ½ tsp baking soda
- ½ tsp salt
- ½ cup (100 g) sugar
- 2 tbsp poppy seeds (optional)
- 1 large egg (beaten)
- 3 fl oz (90 ml) sunflower oil

Orange icing

- ¾ cup (75 g) confectioners' sugar
- 2 tsp grated orange zest*
- 2–3 tsp orange juice
  (*use the zest from the oranges used in the main recipe)

Tools

- 2 x 6-hole or a 12-hole muffin pan
- Paper baking cups
- Grater
- Sharp knife
- Juicer
- Measuring cup
- Large mixing bowl
- Sifter
- Metal spoon
- Fork
- Oven mitts
- Cooling rack
- Small mixing bowl

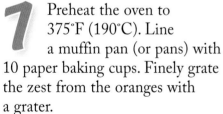

1 Preheat the oven to 375°F (190°C). Line a muffin pan (or pans) with 10 paper baking cups. Finely grate the zest from the oranges with a grater.

2 Cut the oranges in half and squeeze the juice into a measuring cup, removing any seeds. You should have 6 fl oz (180 ml) of orange juice. Add water to make this amount, if necessary.

3 In a large mixing bowl, sift the flour, baking soda, and salt. Stir in the sugar, poppy seeds, and 1 tbsp of the orange zest. Using a metal spoon, mix together.

4 Add the beaten egg and oil to the orange juice and beat together with a fork. Pour the mixture into the bowl and stir until just combined. Don't worry—the batter will be lumpy!

5 Spoon into the baking cups and bake in the center of the oven for 20–25 minutes, until well risen and golden. Leave to cool for a few minutes, then transfer to a cooling rack.

6 Sift the confectioners' sugar into a small bowl, then add the orange zest and juice. Stir until you have a smooth icing. Drizzle over the muffins when they have cooled completely.

Tropical Fruit Cake

This cake is really simple to make. The pineapple and mango add a tropical flavor, but you can use any of your favorite dried fruits.

Variation

This recipe can be made into a traditional fruit cake by replacing the tropical fruit with currants, golden raisins, more raisins, and candied cherries.

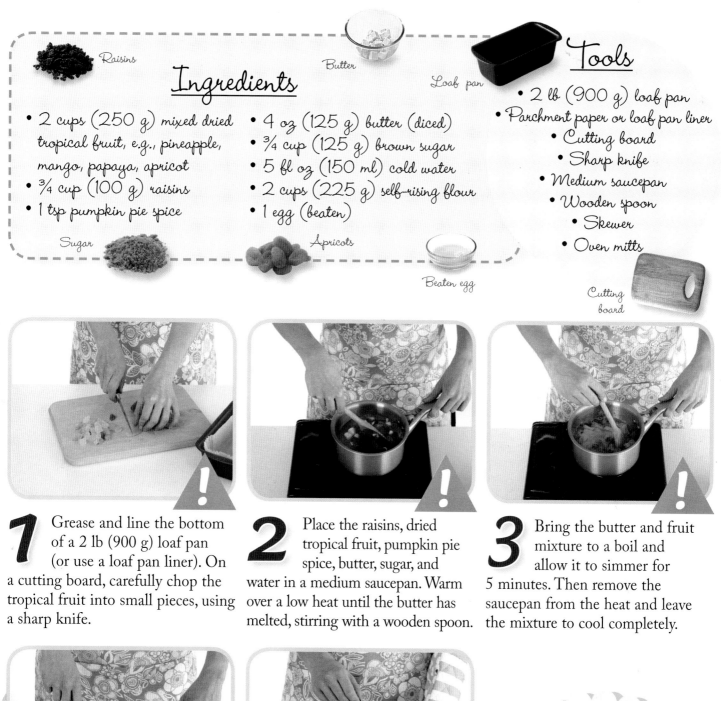

Ingredients

- 2 cups (250 g) mixed dried tropical fruit, e.g., pineapple, mango, papaya, apricot
- ¾ cup (100 g) raisins
- 1 tsp pumpkin pie spice

- 4 oz (125 g) butter (diced)
- ¾ cup (125 g) brown sugar
- 5 fl oz (150 ml) cold water
- 2 cups (225 g) self-rising flour
- 1 egg (beaten)

Raisins

Butter

Loaf pan

Sugar

Apricots

Beaten egg

Tools

- 2 lb (900 g) loaf pan
- Parchment paper or loaf pan liner
- Cutting board
- Sharp knife
- Medium saucepan
- Wooden spoon
- Skewer
- Oven mitts

Cutting board

1 Grease and line the bottom of a 2 lb (900 g) loaf pan (or use a loaf pan liner). On a cutting board, carefully chop the tropical fruit into small pieces, using a sharp knife.

2 Place the raisins, dried tropical fruit, pumpkin pie spice, butter, sugar, and water in a medium saucepan. Warm over a low heat until the butter has melted, stirring with a wooden spoon.

3 Bring the butter and fruit mixture to a boil and allow it to simmer for 5 minutes. Then remove the saucepan from the heat and leave the mixture to cool completely.

4 Preheat the oven to 300°F (150°C). When the mixture is cool, stir in the flour and the egg with the wooden spoon until combined. Then spoon the mixture into the prepared pan.

5 Bake in the center of the oven for 50–60 minutes, or until a skewer inserted into the middle comes out clean. Leave the cake to cool in the pan. When cool, serve in slices.

Chef's Tip

This cake tastes great served in thin slices, spread with a little butter.

85

Lime and Coconut Cupcakes

Medium

Give classic cupcakes a makeover with mouthwatering coconut and refreshing lime.

Makes 18

Prep 10 mins

Cooking 20 mins

Tools

- 12-hole muffin pan
- 6-hole muffin pan
- 18 paper baking cups
- Large mixing bowl
- Electric mixer or whisk
- Metal spoon
- Oven mitts
- Cooling rack
- Small mixing bowl
- Sifter
- Teaspoon

Large mixing bowl

Muffin pan

Sugar

Butter

Ingredients

- 4 oz (125 g) butter (softened)
- 2/3 cup (125 g) sugar
- Finely grated zest and juice of 2 limes
- 2 medium eggs
- 1¼ cups (150 g) self-rising flour
- 1 tsp baking powder
- ¾ cup (50 g) sweetened and dried, desiccated coconut

For the icing
- Grated zest and juice of 1 lime
- 1½ cups (175 g) confectioners' sugar
- A few drops green food coloring (optional)
- 2 tbsp sweetened and dried, desiccated coconut

Eggs

Flour

1 Preheat the oven to 350°F (180°C). Line the muffin pans with 18 paper baking cups. Use two 12-hole muffin pans if you don't have a 6-hole pan or cook the cupcakes in batches.

2 In a large mixing bowl, mix the butter, sugar, and lime zest together using an electric mixer or whisk until they are light and fluffy. Beat in the eggs and lime juice.

3 Using a metal spoon, fold the flour, baking powder, and coconut into the butter and sugar mixture. Divide the mixture between the baking cups. They should be about ⅔ full.

4 Cook the cupcakes in the oven for 15–20 minutes, until well risen and golden (cook them on the top rack if you are cooking in batches). Transfer to a cooling rack and allow to cool.

5 Place ⅔ of the lime zest (saving some for decoration) and lime juice in a bowl and sift over the confectioners' sugar. Stir until the icing is smooth, adding green food coloring if you like.

6 Use a teaspoon to drizzle the icing over the tops of the cooled cupcakes and sprinkle over the coconut. Add the saved curls of lime zest to decorate.

Oat and Honey Muffins

These fluffy light muffins are perfect for breakfast or a midmorning snack because they are packed with nutritious oats and dried fruit.

Muffin pan

Dried apricots

Ingredients

- 2 cups (250 g) all-purpose flour
- 1 tbsp baking powder
- ¾ cup (100 g) rolled oats
- ½ cup (125 g) dried, cooked apricots (chopped)
- ¼ oz (50 g) brown sugar (packed)
- ½ tsp salt
- 2 medium eggs (beaten)
- 6 fl oz (175 ml) milk
- 5 tbsp (75 ml) sunflower oil
- 5 tbsp honey

Tools

- 2 x 6-hole or a 12-hole muffin pan
- 10 paper baking cups
- Large mixing bowl
- Sifter
- Wooden spoon
- Measuring cup
- Fork
- Oven mitts
- Cooling rack

Baking cups

Rolled oats

Honey

Variation

Don't like apricots? Just replace them with your favorite dried fruit, such as papaya or mango.

1 Preheat the oven to 375°F (190°C). Line a muffin pan with 10 paper baking cups. Sift the flour and baking powder into a bowl and stir in the oats, apricots, sugar, and salt.

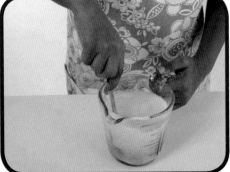

2 Put the flour mixture to one side. In a large measuring cup, beat together the eggs, milk, oil, and honey with a fork until thoroughly mixed and frothy.

3 Pour the wet mixture in the measuring cup over the dry ingredients in the bowl. Stir with a wooden spoon until the ingredients are just combined. The batter will be lumpy and runny.

4 Divide the mixture between the baking cups, so they are ⅔ full, and cook on the top rack of the oven for 20–25 minutes. Leave in the pan for a few minutes, then transfer to a cooling rack.

Chef's Tip
These muffins taste great served with yogurt or fresh fruit and an extra drizzle of honey.

Medium

Makes

15

Prep

10 mins

Cooking

$7\frac{1}{2}$ hours

Cocoa Mint Meringues

These delicious, cocoa-dusted meringues will melt in your mouth—they're crisp on the outside and soft in the middle! They are filled with lightly whipped peppermint cream and chocolate chips.

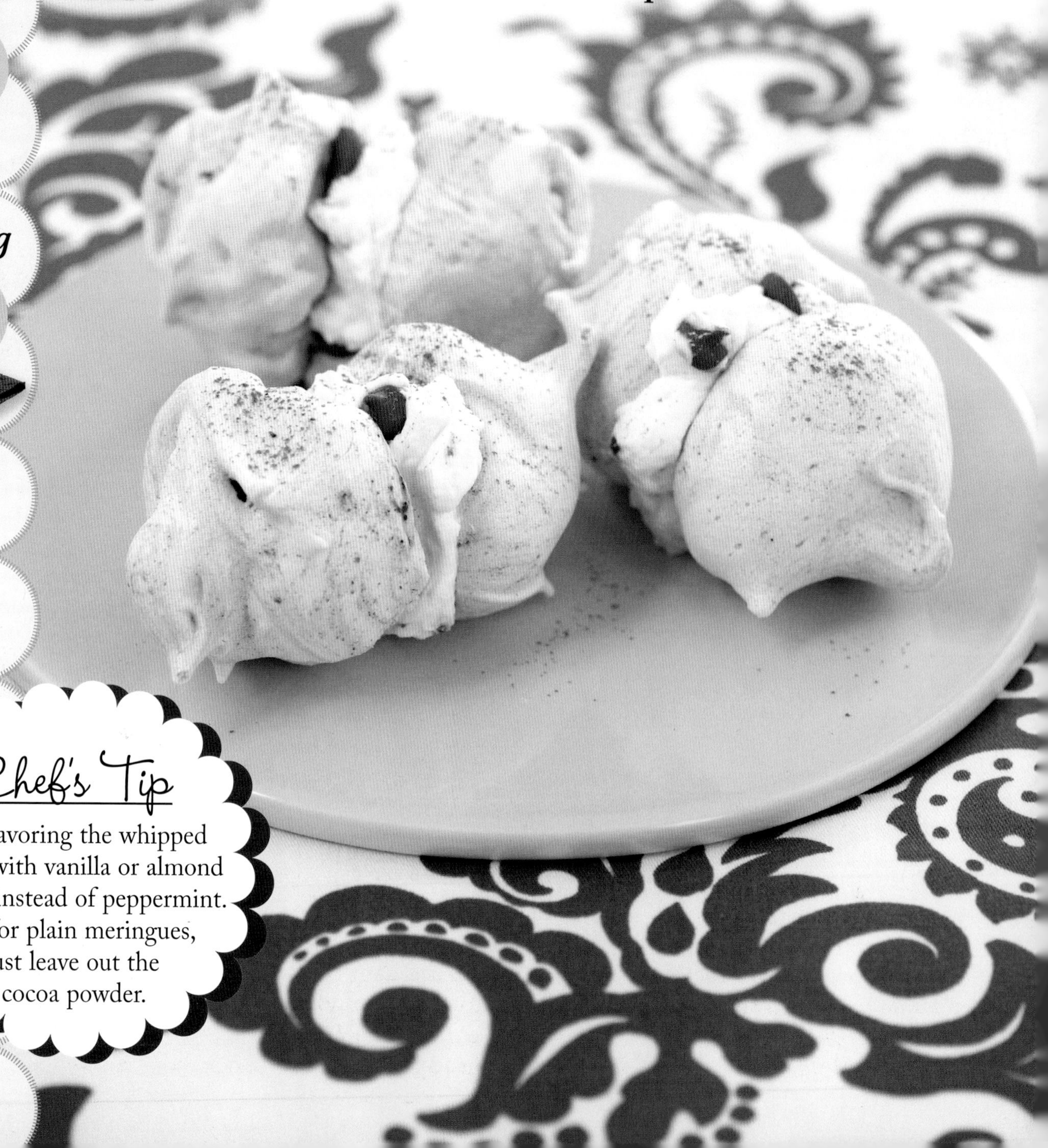

Chef's Tip

Try flavoring the whipped cream with vanilla or almond extract instead of peppermint. Or for plain meringues, just leave out the cocoa powder.

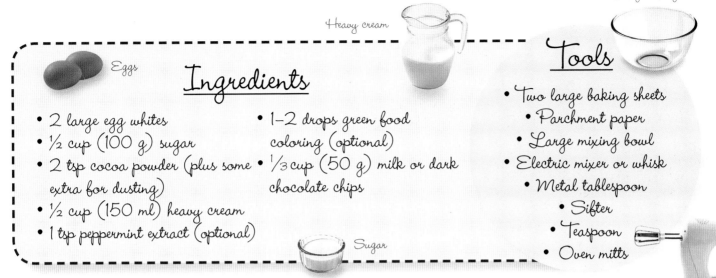

Heavy cream

Large mixing bowl

Eggs

Ingredients

- 2 large egg whites
- ½ cup (100 g) sugar
- 2 tsp cocoa powder (plus some extra for dusting)
- ½ cup (150 ml) heavy cream
- 1 tsp peppermint extract (optional)
- 1–2 drops green food coloring (optional)
- ⅓ cup (50 g) milk or dark chocolate chips

Sugar

Tools

- Two large baking sheets
- Parchment paper
- Large mixing bowl
- Electric mixer or whisk
- Metal tablespoon
- Sifter
- Teaspoon
- Oven mitts

Electric mixer

1 Preheat the oven to 275°F (140°C). Lightly grease two large baking sheets and line with parchment paper. Beat the egg whites in a bowl until they form stiff peaks.

2 Add the sugar to the egg whites a tablespoon at a time, beating well with the electric mixer or whisk after each spoonful. The mixture should be smooth, thick, and glossy.

3 Sift the cocoa powder over the egg white and sugar mixture. Use a metal tablespoon to fold it over a few times until the mixture is streaked. (See page 63 for tips on folding.)

4 Using a teaspoon, place heaps of the mixture onto the prepared baking sheets, spaced a little apart, until you have 30 meringues. Flatten each slightly with the back of the spoon.

5 Bake in the preheated oven for 1½ hours, or until the meringues peel away from the parchment paper without much resistance. Leave them to cool on the baking sheets.

6 Beat the cream, food coloring, and peppermint extract until thick. Stir in the chocolate chips. Spread the mixture on half of the meringues and sandwich with the other halves.

Upside-down Apple Cake

Serves

8–10

Prep

20 mins

Cooking

35 mins

This fruity cake is fun to make and impressive to look at! Rings look prettier, but slices of apple or pineapple also work.

Chef's Tip

Use a sealed cake pan to prevent the cinnamon butter from leaking out over the oven.

1 Preheat the oven to 350°F (180°C). Grease the bottom and sides of an 8" (20 cm) round cake pan, 3" (7.5 cm) deep. The cake pan should not be a springform or loose-bottomed one.

2 Peel the apples with a peeler, then, using a corer, remove the cores from the centers. Cut each apple into 5 rings and place in the bottom of the pan, overlapping if necessary.

Ingredients

Butter

Sugar

Milk

For the topping
- 2 apples
- 2 oz (50 g) butter (diced)
- ¼ cup (50 g) dark brown sugar (packed)
- 1 tsp ground cinnamon (optional)

Eggs

For the cake
- 4 oz (125 g) butter (softened)
- ⅔ cup (125 g) sugar
- 2 large eggs
- 4 fl oz (125 ml) milk
- ½ tsp baking soda
- 1½ cups (175 g) self-rising flour

Tools
- 8" (20 cm) round cake pan with sides 3" (7.5 cm) deep
- Peeler
- Corer
- Sharp knife
- Cutting board
- Small mixing bowl
- Spoon
- Large mixing bowl
- Electric mixer or whisk
- Sifter
- Spatula
- Oven mitts

Cake pan

Peeler

Variation

To make a pineapple upside-down cake, replace the apples with canned pineapple rings in natural juice. Drain the rings well on paper towels and leave out the cinnamon from the topping mixture.

3 In a small mixing bowl, mix together the diced butter, sugar, and cinnamon (if you are using it) and sprinkle the mixture over the apple rings in the bottom of the cake pan.

4 Place the butter and sugar in a large bowl. Using an electric mixer or whisk, beat them together until pale and fluffy. Mix in the eggs, adding a little flour if the mixture starts to curdle.

5 Stir in the milk and baking soda a little at a time, along with some of the flour. Sift in the remaining flour and stir the mixture together until the ingredients are just combined.

6 Pour the cake mixture over the apple rings and spread evenly, using a spatula. Bake the cake in the center of the oven for 30–35 minutes, until golden and firm to the touch.

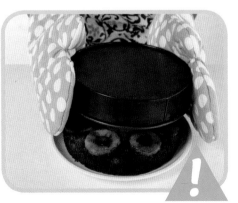

7 Cool the cake in the pan for 5 minutes before removing. Serve the apple upside-down cake in slices. It can be eaten cold or warm, with custard, whipped cream, or ice cream.

Mini Muffins

These bite-sized treats have the delicious combination of tasty banana and melt-in-your-mouth chocolate chips. They are perfect for lunch boxes or for a light snack.

Makes
48

Prep
10 mins

Cooking
12 mins

Ingredients

Sugar
Egg
Butter
Bananas

- 2¼ cups (280 g) all-purpose flour
- 1 tbsp baking powder
- ½ tsp salt
- ⅔ cup (125 g) sugar
- 2 large ripe bananas (peeled and roughly chopped)
- 1 large egg
- 8 fl oz (240 ml) milk
- 3 oz (85 g) butter (melted)
- 1 heaping cup (175 g) milk chocolate chips or chunks

Tools

Fork
Large mixing bowl

- 24-hole mini-muffin pan
- Mini-muffin paper baking cups (optional)
- Large mixing bowl
- Sifter
- Wooden spoon
- Small mixing bowl
- Fork
- Whisk
- Pitcher
- Teaspoon
- Oven mitts

1 Preheat the oven to 400°F (200°C). Grease a 24-hole mini-muffin pan with butter (or line it with mini-muffin paper baking cups) to prevent the muffins from sticking.

2 In a large mixing bowl, sift together the flour, baking powder, and salt. Stir in the sugar with a wooden spoon until all of the ingredients are thoroughly mixed.

3 In a small mixing bowl, mash the two ripe bananas with a fork until nearly smooth, but with a few lumps remaining—this will give the muffins a nice texture.

4 In a pitcher, whisk together the egg, milk, and butter, then pour onto the mashed banana in the bowl. Stir the ingredients together until they are thoroughly combined.

5 Add the egg and banana mixture to the flour mixture. Stir the ingredients together with a wooden spoon until just combined, then fold in the chocolate chips or chunks.

6 Spoon the mixture into the pan and bake for 10–12 minutes. Leave the muffins to cool in the pan, then remove them and repeat with the remaining ingredients to make a second batch.

Baked Raspberry Cheesecake

Serves

8

Prep

15 mins

Cooking

40 mins

Chilling

3¼ hours

This baked cheesecake is so simple to make. You can replace the raspberries with blueberries, if you prefer. Serve at a party for your friends or family.

Variation

Replace the graham crackers with chocolate chip cookies. Delicious!

Ingredients

- 30 (200 g) graham crackers
- 2 oz (50 g) butter
- 2½ cups (600 g) cream cheese
- ²⁄₃ cup (140 ml) sour cream
- 3 tbsp cornstarch
- ¾ cup (75 g) confectioners' sugar
- 3 medium eggs
- 1 tsp vanilla extract
- 2 cups (225 g) fresh raspberries

To serve
- Fresh raspberries
- Confectioners' sugar

Tools

- Plastic food bag
- Rolling pin or food processor
- Cutting board
- Wooden spoon
- Saucepan
- 8" (20 cm) round springform cake pan
- Large mixing bowl
- Electric mixer or whisk
- Metal spoon
- Baking sheet
- Oven mitts

1 Preheat oven to 325°F (170°C). Place the graham crackers in a plastic food bag and crush them with a rolling pin. (You can also do this with a food processor.)

2 Melt the butter in a saucepan; stir in the crushed graham crackers. Press the mixture into the bottom of the pan with the back of a spoon. Chill in the refrigerator for 15 minutes.

3 Place the cream cheese and sour cream in a large mixing bowl. Using an electric mixer or whisk, beat the mixture until smooth. Then beat in the cornstarch and confectioners' sugar.

4 Add the eggs and vanilla extract to the bowl and mix until smooth. Using a metal spoon, carefully stir in the raspberries. Pour this mixture over the graham cracker crust.

5 Place the cake on a baking sheet and bake for 35–40 minutes in the middle of the oven until just set. Leave it to cool, then chill the cake in the refrigerator for 2–3 hours or overnight.

6 Carefully remove the cake from the springform pan and decorate with the fresh raspberries. Dust the cheesecake with confectioners' sugar, and serve it in slices.

Pastry

Pastry is made using flour, fat, and water, and there are many different types of pastry. Puff, shortcrust, and phyllo pastry can be bought fresh or frozen at the grocery store, and work well in the following recipes. If you have time, you can make your own shortcrust pastry using the simple recipe provided.

Different types of pastry

Choux pastry is used for profiterôles and éclairs. Shortcrust pastry is used for making pies and tarts and can be sweet or not. Puff pastry is used for pies and baked goods. Phyllo is lots of thin layers of pastry and is used for sweet and savory pies and tarts.

Top Tip

When rolling out pastry dough, use a cool surface. Dust the surface and rolling pin with a little flour so the dough doesn't stick.

How to make shortcrust pastry

1. In a bowl, sift 1¾ cups (225 g) all-purpose flour with a pinch of salt. Add 4 oz (125 g) diced butter; rub it into the flour using your fingertips.

2. Stir in 3–4 tbsp of cold water with a round-bladed knife until the mixture begins to stick together and form a dough.

3. Knead the dough lightly on a floured work surface until smooth. Wrap it in plastic wrap and chill it for 30 minutes before you use it.

Top Tip

Pastry will be much easier to handle if you make sure your hands are cold when making it. Hot hands will make the butter in the pastry dough melt.

Prebaking

Prebaking is when you bake a pastry crust with dried beans inside it instead of the filling. This seals the pastry and stops it from rising. You then bake it again with the filling inside. If you don't have dried beans, you can use scrunched up aluminum foil.

Chocolate Profiterôles

You won't be able to resist these light and fluffy profiterôles. Topped with warm chocolate sauce, they're simply delicious!

Serves

6

Prep

25 mins

Cooking

25 mins

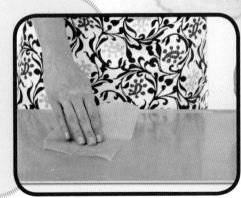

1 Preheat the oven to 400°F (200°C). Grease a baking sheet and sprinkle it with a little cold water. (This will generate steam in the oven and help the choux pastry to rise.)

2 Place the butter and cold water in a medium saucepan and heat gently until the butter has melted. Then turn up the heat and bring the mixture quickly to a boil.

3 Remove the saucepan from the heat and add all the flour at once. Then beat the melted butter and flour together with a wooden spoon until the mixture comes together.

Ingredients

Choux pastry

- 5 fl oz (150 ml) cold water
- 2 oz (50 g) butter (diced)
- ½ cup (75 g) all-purpose flour (sifted)
- 2 medium eggs (beaten)

Filling

- ½ tsp vanilla extract
- 1¼ cups (300 ml) heavy cream

Chocolate sauce

- 4 oz (125 g) dark baking chocolate (broken into small pieces)
- 1 oz (25 g) butter
- 2 tbsp golden syrup, or 1 tbsp corn syrup and 1 tbsp honey

All-purpose flour

Eggs

Saucepan

Large mixing bowl

Chocolate

Tools

- Baking sheet
- Two medium saucepans
- Wooden spoon
- Dessert spoon
- Oven mitts
- Knife
- Electric mixer or whisk
- Large mixing bowl
- Teaspoon
- Heat-proof bowl

Wooden spoon

4 Allow the mixture to cool for a couple of minutes. Then beat in the eggs with an electric mixer or wooden spoon, a little at a time, until the mixture becomes smooth and shiny.

5 Use a dessert spoon to place 12 golf-ball-sized balls of the pastry on the baking sheet. Bake the profiterôles on the top rack of the oven for 20–25 minutes.

6 Using oven mitts, take the cooked profiterôles out of the oven. Make a slit in the side of each with a knife to let the steam out, taking care not to burn your fingers. Allow to cool.

7 Add the vanilla extract and the cream to a large bowl. Whip them to form soft peaks, using the electric mixer or whisk. Then use the teaspoon to spoon the cream into the buns.

8 Place the chocolate, butter, and golden syrup into a heat-proof bowl. Place the bowl over a saucepan of simmering water and gently melt the contents. Stir well.

9 Carefully spoon the chocolate sauce over the profiterôles with a dessert spoon. Then serve immediately with any remaining sauce.

Cherry and Berry Pie

Serves

6–8

Prep

45 mins

Cooking

30 mins

This pie is really easy to make—you simply scrunch up ready-made puff pastry and fill with your favorite berry fruits! You can serve it with a scoop of vanilla ice cream or whipped cream.

Beaten egg

Raspberries

Ingredients

- 18 oz (500 g) ready-made puff pastry
- 1 egg (beaten)
- 2 tbsp semolina
- 4½ cups (650 g) mixed berries, e.g., cherries, blueberries, raspberries, red and black currants
- 2 tbsp sugar
- Confectioners' sugar (for dusting)

Blueberries

Knife

Sugar

Tools

- Rolling pin
- 12" (30 cm) plate
- Sharp knife
- Baking sheet
- Pastry brush
- Teaspoon
- Large mixing bowl
- Large metal spoon
- Oven mitts

Pastry brush

1 Preheat the oven to 400°F (200°C). Roll out the pastry on a lightly floured surface. Cut around a 12" (30 cm) plate with a sharp knife to make a circle.

2 Place the pastry circle on a baking sheet. Use a pastry brush to spread the beaten egg on the pastry, then, using a teaspoon, sprinkle 1 tbsp of the semolina over the pastry.

3 In a large mixing bowl, place the mixed berries, remaining semolina, and 1 tbsp sugar. Use a large metal spoon to mix the ingredients together gently, making sure not to crush the berries.

4 Pile the fruit in the center of the pastry, away from the edge. Scrunch up the edges of the pastry, bringing them toward the center, but leaving the middle exposed.

5 Brush the scrunched-up pastry edges with more beaten egg and sprinkle the pastry with the remaining sugar. Chill for 30 minutes in the refrigerator.

6 Bake the pie on the top rack of the oven for 30 minutes, until golden. If the pastry starts to become too brown, cover the pie with foil. Dust with confectioners' sugar and serve in slices.

Chef's Tip
You can use defrosted frozen berries or any drained canned fruit if fresh berries are not in season.

Chocolate Tart

This is perfect for chocoholics! This chocolate tart has a tangy orange pastry crust. It can be served warm or cold with a dollop of ice cream or whipped cream.

Serves
8

Prep
20 mins

Cooking
45 mins

Variation

Any flavor of jam works well in this recipe and can be substituted for the orange marmalade in Step 3.

1 Preheat the oven to 375°F (190°C). Using a rolling pin, roll out the pastry on a lightly floured surface and use it to line the pie pan. Chill for 15 minutes.

2 Prick the pastry with a fork, line with parchment paper, and fill with dried beans or scrunched-up aluminum foil. Place on the baking sheet and bake on the top rack of the oven for 15 minutes.

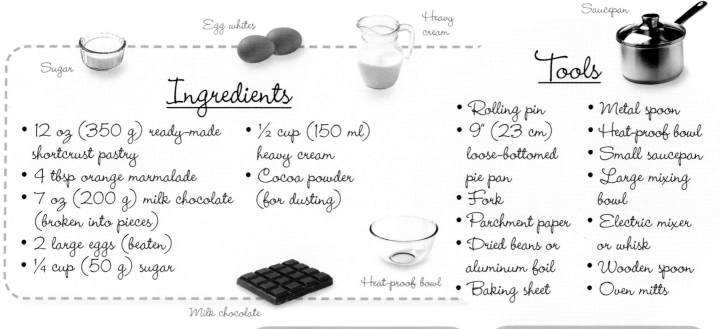

Ingredients

- 12 oz (350 g) ready-made shortcrust pastry
- 4 tbsp orange marmalade
- 7 oz (200 g) milk chocolate (broken into pieces)
- 2 large eggs (beaten)
- ¼ cup (50 g) sugar
- ½ cup (150 ml) heavy cream
- Cocoa powder (for dusting)

Sugar

Egg whites

Heavy cream

Saucepan

Tools

- Rolling pin
- 9" (23 cm) loose-bottomed pie pan
- Fork
- Parchment paper
- Dried beans or aluminum foil
- Baking sheet
- Metal spoon
- Heat-proof bowl
- Small saucepan
- Large mixing bowl
- Electric mixer or whisk
- Wooden spoon
- Oven mitts

Heat-proof bowl

Milk chocolate

Chef's Tip

Placing the pan on a baking sheet will help to make the pastry crust crisp.

3 Remove the paper and beans from the pasty crust and return it to the oven for a further 5 minutes, until golden. While the crust is still warm, spread it with the marmalade.

4 Reduce the oven temperature to 325°F (160°C). Melt the chocolate in a heat-proof bowl over a saucepan of simmering water; stir continuously. Allow to cool slightly.

5 In a large mixing bowl, place the eggs and sugar and beat with an electric mixer or a whisk until pale and fluffy. Stir in the chocolate until thoroughly combined.

6 Stir in the cream with a wooden spoon. Pour the mixture into the crust. Bake for about 25–30 minutes on the top rack of the oven until the tart has just started to set.

7 Remove the tart from the oven. It will continue to set as it cools. Dust with cocoa powder. Serve in slices with a scoop of vanilla ice cream, whipped cream, or crème frâiche.

Lemon Meringue

Serves

6

Prep

10 mins

Cooking

55 mins

This family favorite has a crunchy pie crust layered with a tangy lemon filling and a soft meringue topping. It's a taste sensation!

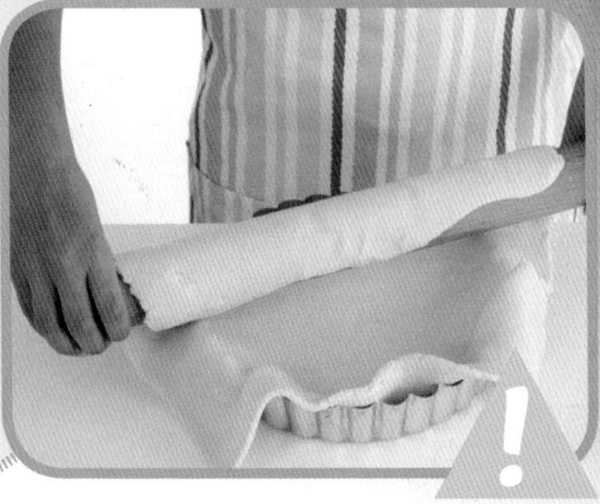

1 Preheat the oven to 375°F (190°C). Roll out the pastry with a rolling pin on a lightly floured surface to about 10" (25 cm). Line the pie pan with the pastry and chill for 15 minutes.

2 Prick the pastry crust with a fork, line with parchment paper, and fill with dried beans or scrunched-up aluminum foil. Place on a baking sheet and bake for 15 minutes.

3 Remove the paper and beans from the pastry crust and return to the oven for a further 5 minutes, until golden. Then reduce the oven to 300°F (150°C).

Lemons

Ingredients

Butter

- 6 oz (175 g) ready-made shortcrust pastry (or see page 99 for a recipe)

For the filling
- 3 tbsp cornstarch
- 5 fl oz (150 ml) cold water
- 2 large lemons

- ⅓ cup (75 g) sugar
- 1 oz (25 g) butter
- 2 large egg yolks

For the topping
- 2 large egg whites
- ½ cup (100 g) sugar

- Rolling pin
- 7½" (19 cm) loose-bottomed pie pan
- Fork
- Parchment paper
- Dried beans or aluminum foil
- Baking sheet
- Oven mitts

- Medium saucepan
- Grater
- Sharp knife
- Cutting board
- Measuring cup
- Wooden spoon
- Large mixing bowl
- Electric mixer or whisk
- Tablespoon

Eggs

Heat-proof bowl

4 Mix the cornstarch and water in the saucepan. Grate the zest from the lemons, cut the lemons in half, and squeeze the juice into a measuring cup, until you have ½ cup (150 ml) lemon juice.

5 Add the lemon zest and juice to the saucepan, then slowly bring to a boil, stirring continuously with a wooden spoon. Simmer, still stirring, until the mixture thickens.

6 Remove the saucepan from the heat and stir in the sugar and butter. Let the mixture cool slightly, then beat in the egg yolks. Pour the mixture into the pie crust.

7 In a clean mixing bowl, beat the egg whites with an electric mixer or whisk until they form stiff peaks. Then stir in the sugar, 1 tbsp at a time, until the mixture is thick and glossy.

8 Spoon the meringue mixture over the lemon mixture, leaving the rim of the pie crust uncovered. Make peaks in the meringue with the back of the spoon, if you like.

9 Place the pie on the top rack of the oven and bake for 30–35 minutes, or until the meringue is crisp and golden. Serve cold or warm with whipped cream or ice cream.

Banoffee Pie

This divinely decadent caramel and banana pie is definitely for those with a sweet tooth!

Serves
8

Prep
20 mins

Cooking
20 mins

Chilling
1½ hours

Chef's Tip
For a really speedy banoffee pie, use a jar of store-bought toffee sauce.

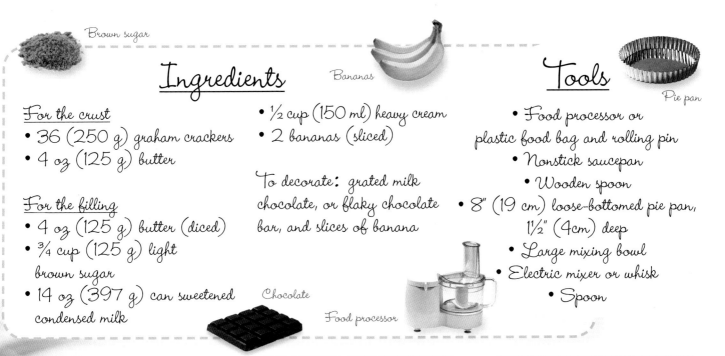

Ingredients

Brown sugar

Bananas

For the crust
- 36 (250 g) graham crackers
- 4 oz (125 g) butter

For the filling
- 4 oz (125 g) butter (diced)
- ¾ cup (125 g) light brown sugar
- 14 oz (397 g) can sweetened condensed milk

- ½ cup (150 ml) heavy cream
- 2 bananas (sliced)

To decorate: grated milk chocolate, or flaky chocolate bar, and slices of banana

Chocolate

Tools

Pie pan

- Food processor or plastic food bag and rolling pin
- Nonstick saucepan
- Wooden spoon
- 8" (19 cm) loose-bottomed pie pan, 1½" (4cm) deep
- Large mixing bowl
- Electric mixer or whisk
- Spoon

Food processor

1 Place the graham crackers in a food processor and process until smooth. If you don't have a food processor, place the graham crackers in a plastic food bag and crush them with a rolling pin.

2 Melt the butter for the crust in a saucepan, then stir in the crushed graham crackers with a wooden spoon. Press the mixture into the crust and sides of the pan. Chill for 30 minutes.

3 Place the diced butter and sugar in the saucepan over a low heat, and stir until the butter has melted. Add the condensed milk and gently bring to a boil, stirring continuously.

4 Boil the butter, sugar, and condensed milk for 5 minutes, stirring continuously until it is a pale caramel color. Pour over the graham cracker crust and chill for 1 hour.

5 In a large mixing bowl, whip the cream with an electric mixer or whisk until it forms soft peaks. Arrange the banana slices over the toffee, then spoon over the whipped cream.

6 Decorate the top of the pie with extra sliced bananas and some grated milk chocolate. Serve the pie in slices. Keep chilled and eat within two days.

Chicken and Ham Potpies

These yummy potpies have tender chicken and ham, cooked in a creamy sauce and topped with golden puff pastry.

Makes

4

Prep

15 mins

Cooking

40 mins

Chef's Tip

If you don't have individual pie dishes, use a large oven-proof dish to make one large pie.

1 Place the butter, flour, stock, and milk in a medium saucepan. Cook over a moderate heat and continue stirring with the whisk until the mixture starts to thicken.

2 Bring to a boil, then reduce the heat and add the crème fraîche and herbs. Season to taste with salt and freshly ground black pepper, then simmer for 2–3 minutes.

3 Heat the oil in a frying pan and add the chicken and onion. Cook for 3–4 minutes, stirring occasionally, until the onion has softened and the chicken has browned.

Ingredients

- 1 oz (25 g) butter
- ¼ cup (25 g) all-purpose flour
- 1 cup (300 ml) chicken stock
- 7 tbsp (100 ml) milk
- 2 tbsp crème fraîche
- 1 tsp dried mixed herbs
- Salt and black pepper
- 1 tbsp vegetable oil
- 1 small onion (sliced)

- 12 oz (350 g) chicken breast (cubed)
- 4 oz (125 g) cooked ham (cubed)
- ¾ cup (100 g) frozen peas
- 12 oz (350 g) ready-made puff pastry
- 1 egg (beaten)

Tools

- Medium saucepan with lid
- Whisk
- Frying pan
- Wooden spoon
- Four individual pie dishes
- Rolling pin
- Sharp knife
- Pastry brush
- Oven mitts

4 Stir the chicken and onions into the sauce, then cover and simmer for 10 minutes. Remove the pan from the heat and stir in the ham and peas.

5 Preheat the oven to 400°F (200°C). Allow the mixture to cool slightly, then divide it between four small, individual pie dishes or fill one large pie dish.

6 Roll out the pastry on a lightly floured surface, then cut out four circles, slightly larger than the tops of the pie dishes. Use the scraps to make thin strips to cover the edges of the pie dishes.

7 Brush the edges of the pie dishes with the egg, then press on the strips of pastry. Brush with egg again, then place the pastry lids on top. Use your fingers to seal the edges of pastry together.

8 Brush the tops with egg and make a cross in the top of each pie to allow the steam to escape. Cook for 20 minutes on the top rack of the oven, until the pastry is puffed and golden.

Variation

Use vegetable stock in Step 1. In Steps 3 and 4, omit the chicken and ham. Simmer the sauce for 5 minutes and add ¾ lb (350 g) cooked potatoes, carrots, and parsnips, and ½ cup (75 g) corn when you add the peas.

Easy

Serves
6

Prep
10
mins

Cooking
20
mins

Tomato and Basil Tart

This tart looks so impressive no one will guess how simple it is to make! Serve it with salad and French bread for a delicious weekend lunch.

Rolling pin

Cutting board

Beaten egg

Tools

- Rolling pin
- Baking sheet
- Sharp serrated knife
- Cutting board
- Large mixing bowl
- Wooden spoon
- Oven mitts

Ingredients

- 12 oz (375 g) ready-made puff pastry
- 9 oz (250 g) cherry tomatoes
- 1 cup (250 g) ricotta cheese
- 2 large eggs (beaten)

- 2 tbsp freshly chopped basil
- 5 tbsp (25 g) Parmesan cheese (grated)
- Salt and black pepper

Cherry tomatoes

1 Preheat the oven to 400°F (200°C). Using a rolling pin on a lightly floured surface, roll out the pastry into a rectangle measuring about 10" x 15" (25 cm x 38 cm).

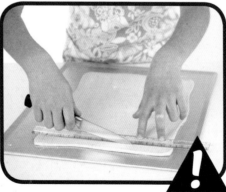

2 Place on a large flat baking sheet and, using a sharp knife, score a 1 in (2.5 cm) border along the sides of the rectangle, being careful not to cut all the way through.

3 Place the cherry tomatoes on a cutting board and use a sharp knife to cut the tomatoes in half. A knife with a serrated edge will make it easier to cut them.

4 In a large mixing bowl, beat together the ricotta cheese, eggs, basil, and Parmesan cheese with a wooden spoon, until combined. Season with a little salt and freshly ground black pepper.

5 Spoon this mixture inside the marked edge and scatter over the tomatoes. Cook in the center of the oven for 20 minutes until the pastry is risen and golden and the filling cooked.

Chef's Tip

To make this recipe even speedier, you could buy ready-rolled puff pastry already in the shape of a rectangle!

Phyllo and Spinach Tarts

The soft and creamy filling contrasts with the light crispy layers of phyllo pastry in this mouthwatering recipe for cheese and spinach tarts.

Variation

Replace the grated cheese with crumbled Feta cheese if you prefer.

Ingredients

Cheese

Beaten egg

- 1 tbsp sunflower oil
- 3½ cups (100 g) baby spinach leaves (washed)
- ½ cup (125 g) cream cheese
- ¼ cup (25 g) Cheddar or Parmesan cheese (grated)

- 1 medium egg (beaten)
- Salt and freshly ground black pepper
- 16 x 5" (2.5 cm) squares phyllo pastry

Salt *Pepper*

Knife

Tools

- Pastry brush
- 6-hole muffin pan
- Cutting board
- Sharp knife
- Large mixing bowl
- Wooden spoon
- Dessert spoon
- Oven mitts

Cutting board

1 Preheat the oven to 350°F (180°C). Use a pastry brush to apply oil to four muffin pan holes. Place the spinach on a cutting board and chop roughly, using a sharp knife.

2 Place the cream cheese in a bowl and beat with a wooden spoon until smooth. Then beat in the grated cheese and egg until combined. Season well, then stir in the spinach.

3 Brush one of the pastry squares with oil. Place another square over the top at an angle to make a star shape. Repeat with two more squares of pastry, brushing each with oil.

4 Gently press the layers of phyllo pastry into one of the holes of the muffin pan, and shape it to fit the hole. Repeat with the remaining pastry until you have four tarts.

5 Use a dessert spoon to fill each pastry crust with the spinach mixture. Press it down with the spoon. Bake for 25 minutes until the pastry has browned and the filling has set.

6 Remove the tarts from the oven and allow them to cool in the pan for a few minutes, then carefully remove them from the pan. Serve hot with salad or vegetables.

Strawberry Tartlets

These pretty tartlets taste as good as they look! Make them when the fruit is in season for the best flavor, although frozen fruit will also work.

Strawberries

Sifter

Ingredients

- 8 oz (225 g) ready-made shortcrust pastry
- ¾ cup (150 g) mascarpone cheese
- ½ tsp vanilla extract
- 2 tbsp confectioners' sugar
- 1¼ cups (175 g) strawberries or other soft fruit
- 4 tbsp red currant gelatin
- 1 tbsp (15 ml) water

Tools

- Rolling pin
- 3½" (9cm) fluted pastry cutter
- Muffin pan
- Eight pieces of aluminum foil
- Oven mitts
- Cooling rack
- Small mixing bowl
- Wooden spoon
- Sifter
- Cutting board
- Sharp knife
- Teaspoon
- Small saucepan
- Pastry brush

Confectioners' sugar

Muffin pan

1 Preheat the oven to 400°F (200°C). Roll out the pastry until it's thin and even; then, using a 3½" (9 cm) fluted pastry cutter, cut out eight circles. Press the pastry circles into a muffin pan.

2 Press a piece of scrunched-up foil into each crust. Cook for 10 minutes, then carefully remove the foil. Return to the oven for 3–4 minutes. Cool in the muffin pan, then transfer to a cooling rack.

3 To make the filling, place the mascarpone cheese and vanilla extract in a small mixing bowl. Sift in the confectioners' sugar, then beat with a wooden spoon until smooth.

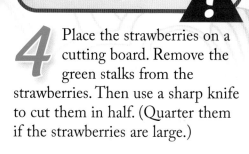

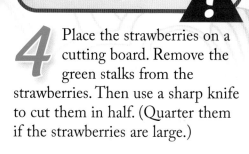

Chef's Tip

Placing scrunched-up foil in the pastry crusts prevents them from shrinking.

4 Place the strawberries on a cutting board. Remove the green stalks from the strawberries. Then use a sharp knife to cut them in half. (Quarter them if the strawberries are large.)

5 When the pastry crusts are completely cool, use a teaspoon to fill them with the mascarpone and vanilla extract mixture. Arrange the strawberries over the top.

6 Place the red currant gelatin in a small pan with the water and cook over a low heat, stirring with a wooden spoon until the gelatin has dissolved. Brush this over the strawberries.

Medium

Apple Crumble

In this twist on a classic dessert, apples are cooked in a rich butterscotch sauce, topped with a crunchy, buttery crumble. Serve with custard or ice cream for the ultimate treat!

Serves

4-6

Prep

20 mins

Cooking

40 mins

Oats

Apples

Ingredients

- 1½ lb (650 g) baking apples
- ½ cup (75 g) light brown sugar
- 1 oz (25 g) butter
- Finely grated zest and juice of ½ lemon
- ¼ tsp salt
- 4 fl oz (100 ml) water

Saucepan

For the crumble
- 1 cup (125 g) all-purpose flour
- 3 oz (75 g) butter (diced)
- 3 tbsp (25 g) oats
- ¼ cup (50 g) sugar

Butter

Tools
- Peeler
- Cutting board
- Apple corer
- Sharp knife
- 1 quart (1 ℓ) oven-proof dish
- Medium saucepan
- Wooden spoon
- Large mixing bowl
- Oven mitts

Corer

Flour

1 Preheat the oven to 350°F (180°C). Using a peeler, peel the apples to remove the skin. Place on a cutting board and use a corer to remove the apple cores.

2 On the cutting board, cut the apples carefully into 1" (2.5 cm) cubes with a sharp knife. Place the pieces in the bottom of an oven-proof dish.

3 Place the sugar, butter, lemon zest and juice, and salt in a saucepan with the water. Bring to a boil, stirring occasionally, until the sugar has dissolved and the butter has melted.

4 Pour the butterscotch mixture over the chopped apples in the oven-proof dish and stir with a wooden spoon until the apples are coated evenly in the sauce.

5 Place the flour in a mixing bowl with the diced butter. Using your fingertips, rub in the butter until the mixture looks like rough crumbs. Stir in the oats and the sugar.

6 Spoon the crumble mixture over the top of the apples and bake in the oven on the top rack for 35–40 minutes, until bubbling and golden. Allow to stand for 5 minutes before serving.

Bacon and Egg Tart

When cooked, the cheese in this bacon and egg tart melts to form a tasty crispy top. Delicious hot or cold, the tart tastes especially good with salad.

Serves
6–8

Prep
20 mins

Cooking
50 mins

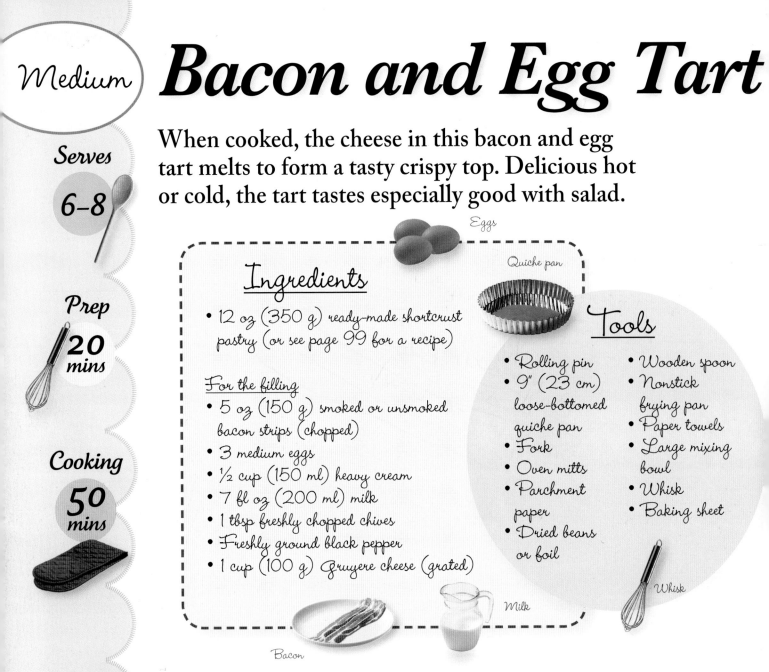

Eggs

Quiche pan

Ingredients

- 12 oz (350 g) ready-made shortcrust pastry (or see page 99 for a recipe)

For the filling
- 5 oz (150 g) smoked or unsmoked bacon strips (chopped)
- 3 medium eggs
- ½ cup (150 ml) heavy cream
- 7 fl oz (200 ml) milk
- 1 tbsp freshly chopped chives
- Freshly ground black pepper
- 1 cup (100 g) Gruyere cheese (grated)

Tools

- Rolling pin
- 9" (23 cm) loose-bottomed quiche pan
- Fork
- Oven mitts
- Parchment paper
- Dried beans or foil
- Wooden spoon
- Nonstick frying pan
- Paper towels
- Large mixing bowl
- Whisk
- Baking sheet

Whisk

Milk

Bacon

1 Preheat the oven to 375°F (190°C). Using a rolling pin, roll out the pastry on a lightly floured surface. Line the loose-bottomed quiche pan with the pastry. Chill for 15 minutes.

2 Prick the dough with a fork, line with parchment paper, and fill with dried beans or scrunched-up foil. Bake for 15 minutes. Remove the paper and beans; bake for another 5 minutes.

3 Meanwhile, place the bacon in a nonstick frying pan and cook over a medium heat, stirring occasionally until it is crisp. Drain the bacon on paper towels.

4 In a large mixing bowl, whisk together the eggs, cream, milk, chives, and freshly ground black pepper with a whisk until they are thoroughly combined.

5 Place the quiche pan with the dough on a baking sheet. Spread the cooked bacon and half the cheese in an even layer in the pan. Pour in the egg mixture; sprinkle with the remaining cheese.

6 Place the tray in the oven and bake on the center rack for 25–30 minutes, until golden and set. Allow to cool for 5 minutes before serving in slices with salad.

Variation

For a cheese-and-onion tart, omit the bacon. Instead, cook a sliced onion in a little oil until softened and scatter over the dough.

Decoration

No cake is complete without some pretty decoration! Whether you use healthy fruit or indulgent icing, here are some top tips for perfect prettiness.

Chef's Tip

Add your liquids, such as water or food coloring, to the confectioners' sugar one drop at a time. You can always add more, but if you add too much it will become too runny.

How to make glaze icing

1 Sift 2 cups (225 g) confectioners' sugar into a mixing bowl. Use your hand or a spoon with the sifter.

2 Gradually stir in 2–3 tbsp of hot water. Add a drop of food coloring if you are using it.

How to make buttercream icing

1 Place 3 oz (75 g) butter in a bowl and beat with a wooden spoon until it has softened.

2 Gradually sift in 1½ cups (175 g) confectioners' sugar. Beat it with a wooden spoon.

3 Beat in 1–2 tbsp milk and/or flavoring until you have a fluffy consistency.

How to make a piping bag

1 Cut out a triangle (i.e., half a square) of parchment paper. Point the long side away from you and fold the right-hand point over.

2 Fold the left-hand point over the cone, bringing all three points together and fold over to secure it in place.

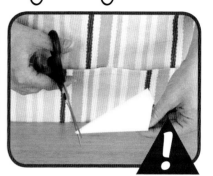

3 Snip off the end with a pair of scissors to create the hole. Put your icing inside the cone and squeeze it out onto the cake. Test it first!

Variations

Here is a selection of cake decorations. They include: sprinkles, sugar flowers, candy-coated chocolates, and mini marshmallows.

Glossary

This is the place to find extra information about the baking terms and techniques used in this book.

B

batch: the group of baked goods that are made; cookies and other baked goods are usually made in more than one batch if there are not enough pans or enough space in the oven.

beat: to stir or mix quickly until smooth, in order to break down or add air.

boil: to heat a liquid, such as water, to a very hot temperature so that it bubbles and gives off steam.

C

chill: to cool in a refrigerator.

combine: to mix ingredients together.

consistency: how runny or thick a mixture is.

cream: to beat butter and sugar together to add air, resulting in a fluffy texture.

curdle: when the liquid and solid parts of an ingredient or mixture separate. Milk curdles when overheated and cakes can curdle if the eggs are too cold or added too quickly.

D

dissolve: to melt or liquify a substance (often sugar in water).

drizzle: to pour slowly, in a trickle.

dough: the mixture of flour, water, sugar, salt, and yeast (and maybe other ingredients) before it is baked into bread.

E

elastic: a mixture with a stretchy texture.

F

fold: to mix ingredients together gently, to retain as much air in the mixture as possible.

frosting: a topping that is usually a creamy icing.

G

grease: to rub butter onto a baking sheet or pan to prevent the baked item from sticking.

H

hollow: something that is empty. Bread sounds hollow when cooked.

I

individual: a single one, or enough for one person.

K

knead: to press and fold the dough with your hands until it is smooth and stretchy. This distributes the yeast and helps dough to rise.

L

level: to make the surface of something the same height.

M

melt: to heat a solid substance until it becomes liquid.

moist: something that is slightly wet.

P

peaks: raised areas that look like the tops of mountains.

prebaking: weighing down a pastry base with dried beans or foil to stop it from rising during baking.

preheat: to turn the oven on and heat it to the correct temperature before baking in it.

process: to blend an ingredient or ingredients in a food processor.

punch down: to deflate risen dough with a gentle punch. This evens out the texture of the bread.

Q

quantity: the amount of an ingredient you need.

R

rich: strongly flavored.

ripe: when a fruit is soft and ready to eat.

S

sandwich: to stick two sides or halves together, usually with a mixture in between.

savory: something that does not taste sweet.

serrated: the edge of a knife that has "teeth."

sift: to use a strainer or sifter to strain a dry ingredient and remove lumps.

simmer: to cook over a low heat so the liquid or food is bubbling gently but not boiling.

skewer: a metal or wooden stick with a sharp end.

sprinkle: to scatter a food lightly over another food.

T

texture: the way something feels, e.g., soft, smooth, chunky, moist, etc.

transfer: to move something from one place to another.

trimmings: pieces of dough or pastry left over after cutting out shapes.

W

well: a dip made in some flour in which to crack an egg or pour liquid.

whisk: to mix ingredients together evenly with a whisk.

Y

yeast: a type of fungus that when added to flour, water, sugar, and salt ferments and causes the mixture to rise.

Z

zest: the peel of a citrus fruit that has been grated with a grater or zester.

Index